PRACTICING

HINDUISM

A Step-by-Step Guide

For The New Generation

By

Sumita Sharma Kolppa

Published by Hemingway Publishers

Cover design by Hemingway Publishers

ISBN: Printed in the United States

Journey Through The Chapters

Embark on a journey through several ancient meditation techniques that have illuminated the paths of spiritual seekers for centuries.

In this chapter, you will learn the true essence of yoga, delving deeper than physical postures to uncover its holistic nature.

Learn the significance of fasting in Hindu tradition, different types of fasts, and how to observe them properly in alignment with spiritual goals.

Discover the meaning behind each festival celebration and follow step-by-step rituals to honor the divine celebration. By following these outlined steps, you can practice the rituals on your own, allowing you to engage in these joyous events fully.

While many Hindu traditions and festivals are celebrated across different regions and countries, this book focuses on the Hindu traditions, festivals, and rituals of Punjab, India.

About the Author

Join me on a transformative journey from the mystical lands of Punjab, India, to the vibrant canvas of Canada, where my life has been an ongoing evolution marked by resilience, growth, and profound learning. My journey began when I moved from India to Canada as a young doctor, facing new cultural challenges. Despite enduring adversity, including abuse and a fractured marriage, I persevered, evolving into a strong woman recognized as a Woman of Distinction and Woman of Color in Canada. I embraced physical and mental strength through fitness, achieving accolades like Miss Canada and Miss North America, yet my aspirations reached beyond these achievements.

Fueled by an inner flame, I ventured into the domain of healing and medicine again, caring for newborns' hearing. The journey seamlessly led me into the spiritual realms of yoga, meditation, and the rich tapestry of Hindu traditions—an expedition in pursuit of life's profound purpose. Soon, Life opened a beautiful chapter of love and marriage for me. I found profound joy in raising my children with a harmonious blend of Indian and Western traditions. As my children began to embrace the rhythms of adult life in the Western world, a profound realization dawned. The essence of Hinduism, integral to my identity, seemed to be slipping away from them. That was the pivotal moment when I sensed a profound responsibility to safeguard my Hindu heritage.

To anchor Hindu traditions and teachings, I founded Healing Movements Yoga Centre. In this sanctuary, Hindu spiritual practices and teachings thrived amidst the challenges of a bustling Western world. However, as the center expanded and shifted focus to profitability over spiritual healing and teachings, I chose to step back from leadership. Redirecting my efforts, I dedicated myself to reinvigorating the profound teachings of Hinduism within my family. I am steadfast in ensuring that my children and future generations embrace and preserve this invaluable heritage and its timeless wisdom. Through this book, I aim to empower, foster and pass on the rich traditions and teachings of Hinduism to the next generation.

This book will remain a guide, to instill the Hindu values and traditions, whether they are embraced now or later.

In this book, each page resonates with the enduring beauty of Hindu culture a legacy worth cherishing and passing on to new generations. Your support is not just for a book but for a living tradition, inviting you to embrace the flame we, Hindus, carry and ensure it lights the way for those who come after.

I Pass the Flame to You,

Sumita

Dedication

In Loving Memory of My Beloved Grandma Smt. Satya Wati. Her Enduring Legacy of Wisdom and Hindu Traditions Lives On.

This book is a heartfelt tribute to the treasured memory of my dear grandmother, whose enduring grace, wisdom, and teachings have woven a timeless tapestry of love and tradition into the fabric of my life. She devoted her life to God during her teenage years when she faced the challenges of being a widow and the responsibility of raising two young children on her own a remarkable accomplishment, especially considering the circumstances over a century ago. Yet, she navigated this path with resilience, offering physical and material support and sharing the wealth of her wisdom, cultural stories, and traditions with her children and grandchildren. I hold her in my heart, missing her dearly.

With every page turned in this book, I lovingly honour her legacy and the profound love she showered upon me. This book serves as a vessel, carrying forward the invaluable lessons she imparted, ensuring that her wisdom and love endure for generations to come.

With heartfelt love and eternal gratitude,

Sumita

Chapter 1

Introduction to Hinduism

In the sacred soil of ancient India, Hinduism began like a big, old tree growing slowly over thousands of years. Imagine it as a magical tree with a rich history, a history that represents the beliefs of Hindus, a history that explains the culture of Hinduism, and a history that is the reason for the prevalence of this diverse religion and community. This magical tree does not have an end. It keeps growing and will last until the last member of this vast community lives on the planet.

Long ago, in ancient cities, people left symbols hinting at spiritual practices, like pieces of an ancient story waiting to be discovered. These pieces were scattered all over the place, narrating the story. Then came the Indo-Aryans, bringing special texts called the Vedas. These texts were like the roots of the tree, giving Hinduism its first teachings and rituals. These texts gave birth to Hinduism and brought the first-ever version of this versatile religion to the world.

During a time of great stories, like epics, wise teachings appeared in the Mahabharata and Ramayana. Any true Hindu would know what these tales are. These sacred stories explain the life journeys of some of the – most prominent Hindu Lords and Deities. More stories followed in the Puranas, adding new layers to the tree with deities and rituals. People built temples and started doing more rituals, making this tree even more vibrant. Now, this tree had its branches spreading all over the place. More and more people were learning about this tree, which brought more believers to the religion.

In the Gupta Empire's time, creativity bloomed, adding colorful flowers to the tree. The Bhakti movement came along, saying it's not just about rituals; you can have a personal connection with the divine. So, with each development, this tree grew well and attracted preachers.

Like an old wise tree with roots deeply embedded in ancient cities, Hinduism extends its branches, brimming with timeless stories, and unfurls blossoms of creativity through the ages. It keeps growing and changing, making room for everyone to find their own way in this special garden of spirituality. It serves as a spiritual touchstone, fostering connections among people and guiding them to build a deeper relationship with the divine and discover their true origins.

Key Periods of Hinduism

Hinduism, evolving over thousands of years, has a rich history shaped by key periods. These key periods help identify the major developments throughout the history of Hinduism and how they affected the people who followed the religion.

Indus Valley Civilization (3300–1300 BCE)

Symbols on artifacts hint at early roots in the ancient Indus Valley. The history of the Indus Valley Civilisation lies in the artifacts that were discovered later on. Among these artifacts, there were signs and symbols that identified that the people of the civilization praised and worshiped different Gods, which were discovered to be the Hindu Gods.

Vedic Period (1500–500 BCE)

Indo-Aryans introduced the Vedas, laying the foundation for Vedic practices. From 1500 BCE to 500 BCE, the Vedic period marked the arrival of Aryan tribes in India, shaping its early civilization. The Vedas, composed during this time, are foundational texts of Hinduism, containing hymns, rituals, and philosophical insights. Hinduism emerged from Vedic beliefs, with core concepts like dharma, karma, and moksha. Worship of multiple deities, reincarnation, and moral conduct became central tenets.

Upanishadic Thought (800–200 BCE)

The Upanishads, composed between 800 BCE and 200 BCE, marked a significant shift in Vedic thought. They delved into profound philosophical inquiries, introducing concepts like Brahman (ultimate reality), Atman (individual soul), Maya (illusion), Karma (law of cause and effect), and Moksha (liberation). These ideas influenced the development of Hinduism, particularly Vedanta, emphasizing the unity of Atman with Brahman. The Upanishads challenged ritualism, promoting introspection and meditation for spiritual realization.

Epic Period (500 BCE–200 CE)

Mahabharata and Ramayana conveyed moral teachings; Bhagavad Gita provided profound insights. These epics, while showcasing heroic narratives and moral teachings, also incorporate philosophical and theological ideas central to Hinduism. The Mahabharata contains the Bhagavad Gita, a sacred text presenting a dialogue on duty, righteousness, and devotion, profoundly influencing Hindu thought. The Ramayana narrates the life and adventures of Lord Ram, embodying ideals of dharma and virtue. These epics played a crucial role in popularizing Hinduism and continue to be revered as sources of moral and spiritual guidance.

Post-Epic and Puranic Period (200 BCE–500 CE)

Hindu traditions expanded, and Puranas popularized tales and temple rituals. This period saw the flourishing of the Hindu Puranas, ancient texts recounting tales of gods, goddesses, and legendary figures. These texts played a significant role in shaping Hindu religious beliefs and practices, expanding the pantheon of deities, and providing narratives for rituals and festivals.

Gupta and Post-Gupta Period (300–1200 CE)

The Gupta Empire saw artistic flourishing, diverse temples, and the rise of bhakti devotion. This period is often regarded as the golden age of Hinduism. Under Gupta rule, Hinduism experienced a revival, with temples constructed, religious literature produced, and philosophical ideas refined. The period saw the consolidation of Hindu religious practices, the flourishing of Sanskrit literature, and the codification of Hindu law. After the Gupta period decline, the post-Gupta period (6th to 12th century CE) witnessed the spread of Bhakti movements and the emergence of regional kingdoms, fostering diverse – religious expressions within Hinduism.

Medieval and Bhakti Movement (600–1700 CE)

The Bhakti movement emphasized a personal connection with the divine; saints like Kabir made Hinduism accessible. Bhakti saints like Ramanuja, Madhv-acharya, and Chaitanya Mahaprabhu advocated for a more accessible and inclusive form of worship, transcending caste and societal barriers. Their teachings catalyzed social reform and cultural revitalization, contributing to the resilience and adaptability of Hinduism amidst challenging times.

Core Concepts of Hinduism

The Core Concept of Hinduism is doing the right thing (dharma), that your actions have consequences (karma), and that everyone's goal is to be free from the cycle of life and rebirth (moksha). It is a pretty straightforward approach. If you do good, you get good. If you do bad, you will have to face the bad karma. Hinduism truly believes in the concept that whatever is happening to you is because of your deeds. So, basically, what you sow is what you reap.

The Concept of Dharma and Karma

"Dharma" means duty, and Hinduism is called "Sanatana Dharma" because it refers to God's eternal duty. This duty isn't exclusive to Hindus; it extends to everyone, including gods. Each living being in God's creation has a unique role and duty. Everyone shares this eternal duty, regardless of who they are, both now and in the future.

Animals, like dogs or snakes, instinctively play their roles in nature. While divine beings, or gods, ensure the universe's order, guiding natural elements in their roles. Human duties center around preserving order by nurturing gods, ancestors, those in need, and other living beings. These responsibilities are pivotal for fostering harmony, peace, and cosmic order.

"Dharma" is like a life guide, helping us do our duties and act with principles to keep the world in order. Our Individual duties vary based on birth, circumstances, and chosen professions. Ideally, pursuing a profession aligned with one's passion is recommended. Regardless, sincerity and dedication are essential, as every action impacts others and the world.

Now, "karma" is the idea that our actions have consequences. If we do our duties well (good karma), it leads to positive outcomes. If we don't, it might bring negative consequences (bad karma). Think of it as a cosmic balance sheet – doing good adds positive points, and doing the opposite adds negatives. The aim is to build up positive karma by living in harmony with our duties. This creates a positive path for ourselves and the world.

Remember that animals live for themselves, and gods exist for others, but humans have a choice. We can live selfishly or selflessly, expressing the divinity within us. Our lifestyle is a distinctive opportunity that shapes our present and future. Exploring and Embracing Hindu Beliefs not only preserves our heritage but also instills essential life lessons, nurturing a more compassionate and culturally aware generation.

The Concept of Moksha

Hinduism believes in the essence of Brahman, a formless cosmic spirit present everywhere. Within each individual resides (Soul) Atman, a divine spark connected to Brahman's pure essence. This emphasizes the universal link between every soul and the cosmic spirit.

As we progress through our journey, we encounter the captivating illusion of Maya, a deceptive concept that tricks our senses into seeing the material world as the ultimate reality. The spiritual journey often involves transcending Maya's illusions to gain a deeper understanding of the eternal reality – represented by the cosmic spirit, Brahman.

Life unfolds as the rhythmic dance of Samsara, a continuous cycle of existence involving birth, life, death, and rebirth, providing – numerous opportunities for the soul to learn and grow. Samsara, the journey of the soul through various lives, intertwines with reincarnation, the process where the soul adopts different bodies in each life.

When a person dies, the soul is reborn into a new body, starting a fresh life. This cycle of rebirth persists until the soul achieves spiritual enlightenment, breaking free from the cycle and attaining Moksha.

A Guru (teacher) is vital on this spiritual journey, serving as a beacon of wisdom. The Guru guides the seeker through different paths, such as the path of Yoga and Meditation, which unites the individual soul with the cosmic spirit, harmonizing body, mind, and spirit. The practice of Puja creates a heartfelt connection to the divine through rituals and offerings. Additionally, Bhakti, the path of devotion, weaves a tapestry of love and surrender to the cosmic spirit. The Guru illuminates these paths, helping the seeker navigate and integrate them on their journey toward spiritual growth and ultimate liberation from the cycle of rebirth.

A Hindu Home: Living the Hindu Way

"Hindu living" encompasses a rich tapestry of cultural, spiritual, and ethical practices that guide individuals in their daily lives. While practices may vary among individuals and communities, here are some key aspects often associated with Hindu living.

Dharma (Righteous Duty)

Living in accordance with one's dharma involves fulfilling one's duties and responsibilities based on societal roles, age, and personal circumstances. Dharma is seen as a moral and ethical compass, emphasizing the importance of upholding righteousness, justice, and harmony in one's actions and interactions with others. It guides individuals in making decisions that align with honesty, integrity, compassion, and fairness principles, fostering a strong sense of moral and ethical duty towards oneself, others, and the larger community.

Family and Community Values

Hindu living places a strong emphasis on family and community. It's not just about individual practices but about being part of a larger whole. Respect for elders, strong family bonds, and active participation in community events are often integral to the Hindu way of life, fostering a sense of connection and belonging.

Rituals and Worship

Hindus incorporate daily rituals, prayers, and worship (puja) into their routine. These practices, which often involve personal or family prayers and the use of home temples featuring images or idols of deities, are not just routine but a way to maintain a spiritual connection and discipline. For most families, the day begins and ends with the puja, and all practicing Hindus also make sure to visit temples every now and then, further strengthening their spiritual connection.

Festivals and Celebrations

Hindus celebrate a multitude of festivals throughout the year, each with its own significance. These festivals are occasions for joy and religious observance, strengthening social bonds within the community and fostering a deep sense of celebration and religious devotion.

Vegetarianism

While not universally followed, most Hindus practice vegetarianism to express compassion for all living beings. The belief in ahimsa (non-violence) is a key factor influencing dietary choices. By following a vegetarian diet, Hindus seek to foster a sense of respect and reverence for life. Additionally, a vegetarian diet is believed to promote physical health, mental clarity, and spiritual well-being, aligning with the holistic principles of Hindu living.

Yoga and Meditation

Hindu philosophy includes practices like yoga and meditation, which promote physical, mental, and spiritual well-being. These practices are often integrated into daily routines for self-discovery and inner peace. Yoga, with its various asanas (postures), pranayama (breathing techniques), and dhyana (meditation) serves as a holistic approach to maintaining balance and harmony in life. These disciplines not only enhance physical health and mental clarity but also facilitate spiritual growth, allowing individuals to transcend the material world and experience deeper states of consciousness.

Pilgrimages

Visiting sacred sites and undertaking pilgrimages to revered places are standard practices for Hindus seeking spiritual growth and divine blessings. These journeys often involve rituals, prayers, and acts of devotion, creating opportunities for deep reflection and a stronger connection to the divine. Through these sacred travels,

Hindus immerse themselves in the rich tapestry of their faith, reinforcing their spiritual beliefs and cultural heritage.

Astrology and Auspicious Timing

Hindu living often considers astrology for auspicious timings (muhurta) for important events or the start of new endeavors. This practice extends to daily life decisions, including naming children, purchasing property, and undertaking significant journeys, reflecting the deep interconnection between cosmic influences and personal destiny in Hindu tradition.

Cultural Arts

Hindu culture is rich in artistic expressions like classical dance, music, and traditional arts. These forms of expression are not only appreciated for their aesthetic value but also hold spiritual significance. Classical dances like Bharatanatyam and Kathak tell stories from ancient scriptures, while music forms like Carnatic and Hindustani evoke devotional themes and moods. Traditional arts such as rangoli and intricate temple carvings reflect the divine and are often created as offerings to deities. These artistic practices serve as a means to connect with the divine, preserve cultural heritage, and express the spiritual beliefs and values that underpin Hindu life.

Education and Knowledge

The pursuit of knowledge, both secular and spiritual, is highly valued in Hinduism. Learning from sacred texts, scriptures, and philosophical teachings is considered an essential aspect of life. This quest for understanding encompasses studying the Vedas, Upanishads, and Bhagavad Gita, which offer profound insights into the nature of existence, ethics, and the path to enlightenment. Additionally, disciplines such as Ayurveda, astrology, and classical literature contribute to a holistic approach to wisdom. This commitment to knowledge fosters intellectual growth, ethical living, and spiritual advancement, guiding individuals toward a more enlightened and fulfilling life.

Guidelines for Respect and Reverence in Hinduism

Hinduism centers around the principle of respect, guiding individuals to live with purpose, balance, and morality. Respect is integral to every aspect of Hindu living, shaping how one connects with divine energy and sacred traditions. Spiritual practices and daily routines are designed to honor these core beliefs. Adhering to these practices and avoiding actions that compromise spiritual integrity are expressions of respect. They ensure that every moment aligns with the profound values of Hinduism and maintains a sacred connection to its eternal truths. This holistic approach to respect and spirituality transforms daily actions into expressions of reverence and devotion, enriching one's spiritual journey and honoring the essence of Hinduism. Here are respectful guidelines based on Hinduism, crafted to honor its core principles and sacred traditions.

Respect for Cows: Recognize that cows are revered in Hinduism as symbols of motherhood, providers of essential resources like milk, and sacred beings mentioned in Hindu scriptures. Respecting cows aligns with the principle of non-violence (ahimsa), as harming them contradicts this value. Their economic importance and association with blessings and prosperity further underscore their sacred status. The celestial cow Kamdhenu, believed to be the mother of all cows, embodies these virtues as a divine wish-fulfilling entity that grants abundance and spiritual blessings. The reverence for cows is further emphasized in the stories of Lord Krishna, who, known as the protector of cows, spent his childhood tending them in Vrindavan. This highlights their sanctity and integral role in both spiritual and pastoral life.

Respect for Food: Understand that wasting food is strongly discouraged in Hindu culture, as it is considered disrespectful. This practice underscores the value of food and the importance of conserving resources, reflecting a profound respect for the sustenance provided by nature. Food is seen as a gift from the divine and a vital element of life, deserving of gratitude and mindful consumption. By minimizing waste and appreciating every morsel, individuals honor the effort that goes into producing and preparing food and the natural resources that sustain life. This respect for food aligns with broader ethical principles of stewardship and gratitude, reinforcing a commitment to living in harmony with the environment and acknowledging the divine in everyday blessings.

Respect for Religious Items: Avoid stepping over religious items such as idols, sacred texts, or ritual objects. Doing so is considered impolite and deeply disrespectful because these items are seen as sacred representations of the divine and hold profound spiritual significance. Such actions can be interpreted as a disregard for the sanctity of these objects, which are revered as symbols of divine presence and spiritual teachings. To honor their sacred nature, always treat these items with utmost care and respect. Ensure they are placed in appropriate, clean spaces and handled with reverence, acknowledging their role in spiritual practice and devotion. This respect reflects a broader commitment to honoring the divine and upholding the values of faith and reverence.

Respect for Personal Space: Do not walk over someone who is sitting or lying down. In Hinduism, this action is considered deeply disrespectful, as it can disturb the person's space and energy. Walking over someone is seen as an intrusion into their personal space and disrupting their spiritual and physical well-being. This consideration not only honors their presence but also maintains harmony in the environment, reflecting a broader commitment to respect and thoughtful interaction.

Respect for Temple Etiquette: Wear appropriate attire and remove your footwear when entering Hindu temples. This practice demonstrates respect for the sacred space and helps maintain its purity by preventing the entry of impurities from outside.

Appropriate attire usually involves modest clothing that covers the shoulders and knees, reflecting the reverence and sanctity of the temple environment. Removing footwear is symbolic of leaving behind worldly concerns and entering a space dedicated to spiritual practice and divine worship. This ritual not only upholds the cleanliness of the temple but also signifies a respectful approach to the divine presence. By observing these customs, individuals honor the sacredness of the space and participate in the spiritual tradition that underscores humility, respect, and devotion.

Respect for Elders: In Hindu culture, it is highly valued to show respect to parents and elders. It is customarily considered respectful not to address them by their names, honoring their position and wisdom within the family. This practice reflects deep gratitude and reverence for their life experience and guidance. Respecting elders also involves seeking their advice, listening attentively, and following their teachings, which are seen as vital for personal growth and maintaining family harmony. Additionally, physical gestures – such as touching their feet as a sign of reverence further symbolize respect and humility. By upholding these customs, individuals demonstrate their commitment to family values and the cultural importance of honoring those who have paved the way with their wisdom and experience.

Respect for Energy: In Hinduism, hair is believed to play a crucial role in channelling and harmonizing one's spiritual and energetic well-being. Therefore, cutting hair is approached with care, often done on days determined by lunar cycles or specific rituals, to align personal energy with cosmic harmony.

Similarly, customs regarding nail cutting reflect these spiritual beliefs. It is advised to avoid washing and cutting nails and hair on certain days of the week, such as Tuesdays, Thursdays and Saturdays because this displeases the planets and deities governing these days. Additionally, cutting nails at night is generally avoided to prevent the invitation of negative energies or disruption of spiritual peace. These practices highlight a deep respect for religious observances and the belief that maintaining proper timing helps preserve both personal and universal energy. By following these customs, individuals honor traditional wisdom and seek to live in alignment with spiritual and energetic principles.

NOTE: It's also crucial to recognize the diversity within Hindu living, as individuals interpret and practice these aspects differently, influenced by personal beliefs, regional customs, and family traditions. Despite these variations, the essence remains consistent: an earnest pursuit of harmony with oneself, others, and the divine throughout life's profound journey.

Chapter 2

Exploring Gods and Goddesses of Hinduism

Hinduism is a vast and diverse religion where devotees may worship one or multiple deities, all seen as manifestations of Parabrahman, the Supreme Reality beyond shape and form. Ishvara, representing this ultimate reality, is worshipped as the divine essence. Some followers choose havans (fire rituals) over deity worship as a direct means to commune with Ishvara. Additionally, some devotees worship Ishvara through manifested forms such as devas and devis, recognizing them as divine manifestations that lead to the ultimate realization of truth. Even though there are numerous paths to reach Ishvara, Hindus universally believe that each path leads to the Supreme and the realization of truth.

Hinduism has numerous and diverse deities, ranging from powerful devas (gods) like Brahma, Vishnu, and Shiva to various devis (goddesses) like Durga, Kali, and Saraswati. Each deity has a unique role and significance in Hinduism, representing different aspects of the universe and human life.

Worship of these deities is an integral part of Hindu culture, and it involves the recitation of sacred chants and hymns. These chants have a purifying effect on the mind and soul and help establish a connection with the divine.

In this chapter, we delve into the lives and significance of some popular devas and devis, understanding their responsibilities and the sacred chants.

Brahma Deva - The Creator

Duty of the Deity

Brahma Deva is one of the most revered deities in Hinduism and is known as the creator of the universe. The duty of this deity is to create life in the universe. Brahma is often depicted as the cosmic architect who created the universe and all life within it.

Aspects of the Deity

Brahma's divine nature and cosmic role are reflected through various names and titles.

Vedanta: God of the Vedas.

Hiranyagarbha: The Golden Embryo or the Cosmic Womb.

Prajapati: The God of Progeny or the Creator of All Beings.

Chaturmukha: The Four-Faced One (depicting his four faces representing the four Vedas).

Vedakarta: The Creator of the Vedas.

Svayambhu: Self-existent or Self-born.

Vishvakarma: The Architect of the Universe.

Lokesha: The God of the Worlds.

Vagish: The God of Speech.

Chant Mantra of the Deity

Chant this mantra to honor Brahma and show respect for the gift of life bestowed upon you.

(Om Brahmaya Namah)

Meaning: "I bow to Brahma, the creator."

Divine Form of the Deity

Brahma is often depicted with multiple heads and hands, each carrying specific items.

Four Heads: Brahma is usually shown with four heads. Each represents a cardinal direction, symbolizing his vast knowledge and wisdom and his ability to oversee all creation simultaneously.

Four Arms: Each arm holds different items, representing Brahma's diverse responsibilities.

Rosary (Mala): Those beads represent the ever-turning wheel of time, reminding us that everything in existence is part of a continuous cycle of creation, preservation, and dissolution.

Water Pot (Kamandalu): Filled with the holy waters of creation, this pot symbolizes the very source of life itself. From this vessel springs forth all that exists, reminding us of Brahma's immense power.

Vedas: The sacred texts or books symbolize the foundation of knowledge, wisdom, and learning. In Brahma's hand, they signify his role as the ultimate teacher, bestowing knowledge upon the universe.

Lotus: This beautiful flower symbolizes purity, the unfolding of the universe from the divine, and the potential for growth within every being.

Human Attributes: Amidst all these divine emblems, Brahma's– appearance with human-like features reminds us that despite his grand role, he is connected to humanity and his role as the creator of life and the universe.

Cultivating Connection

To deepen your connection with Brahma, immerse yourself in the profound wisdom of Vedic teachings. Let the timeless principles of the Vedas guide you as you integrate their knowledge into the challenges and rhythms of modern life. By living in alignment with these ancient truths, you will nurture a genuine and lasting relationship with God Brahma, allowing the sacred wisdom of the Vedas to illuminate your everyday experiences.

Om Brahmaya Namah

Saraswati Devi- The Goddess of speech

Duty of the Deity

Saraswati Devi is a revered deity in Hinduism who is the consort of Brahma, the creator deity. According to the Vedas, Saraswati is known as Brahmi or Vak Devi, the goddess of speech, and is considered to be the personification of wisdom and knowledge. It's believed that she emerged from Brahma's mouth at the beginning of the creation of the universe, and together they initiated the task of creation. Saraswati is a multi-faceted goddess, inspiring us with her association with knowledge, wisdom, music, arts, speech, and learning.

Aspects of the Deity

Saraswati, the radiant goddess of knowledge, music, and creativity, isn't confined to a single title. She's a kaleidoscope of divine qualities, each – reflected in the many names and epithets she holds.

Bharati: Signifying eloquence and speech.

Savitri: Associated with the concept of the Sun and representing – enlightenment.

Vakdevi: Goddess of speech.

Vagishvari: Goddess of Knowledge.

Shatarupa: The One with a Hundred Forms.

Brahmi: Associated with the Brahman or cosmic consciousness.

Mahavidya: The One with Great Wisdom and Knowledge.

Each name and title describe different qualities of Saraswati, highlighting her role as the giver of knowledge, creativity, speech, and the arts in Hindu beliefs. People use these names when they pray or perform rituals to seek her blessings and guidance in their pursuit of knowledge and wisdom.

Chant Mantra of the Deity

Chant this mantra to honor Saraswati and invite her divine grace.

(Om Aim Saraswatyai Namah)

Meaning: "I bow to Saraswati, the bestower of wisdom."

Divine Form of the Deity

Saraswati appears graceful and elegant, usually adorned with white attire, representing purity and knowledge.

Four Arms: She has four arms representing aspects of learning and creativity.

Vedas: Symbolizes ancient sacred texts and knowledge.

Veena (Musical Instrument): Depicts the arts and creative expression.

Rosary (Mala): Symbolizes meditation, concentration, and spiritual development.

Lotus: Represents purity, enlightenment, and the unfolding of – knowledge.

Swan: Saraswati is frequently depicted sitting on or close to a swan, symbolizing grace and wisdom. The swan represents the ability to distinguish between right and wrong and the skill to extract the essence of knowledge.

Flowing Water: Sometimes depicted with a stream of water, – emphasizing the continuous flow of wisdom, creativity, and knowledge.

Together, these symbols paint a rich and complex picture of this revered goddess, highlighting her many facets and her deep significance in Hindu traditions and culture.

Cultivating Connection

To honor Goddess Saraswati, embrace a life of truth, wisdom, and eloquent speech. Seek her blessings in your pursuit of knowledge, speaking words of kindness and clarity. Connect with her serene presence through study, reflection, and meditation, allowing her to guide your thoughts and expressions. By living with sincerity and creativity, you cultivate a deep and meaningful bond with Goddess Saraswati.

Om Aim Saraswatyai Namah

Vishnu Deva - The Preserver

Duty of the Deity

In Hinduism, Vishnu is one of the three major deities, along with Brahma and Shiva. Vishnu (Narayana) is known as the Preserver and is responsible for maintaining cosmic balance and restoring righteousness when disturbed.

Aspects of the Deity

One of the most fascinating aspects of God Vishnu is his ability to take on various forms or avatars. These avatars are believed to be incarnations of Vishnu and are said to have manifested to maintain cosmic order and restore righteousness.

Matsya (The Fish Avatar): Manifested to save the sage Manu and the Vedas during a big flood.

Kurma (The Tortoise Avatar): Assumed the form of a turtle to support the Mandara mountain during the churning of the ocean (Samudra–Manthan).

Varaha (The Boar Avatar): Appeared as a boar to rescue the earth goddess, Bhudevi, from the demon Hiranyaksha, who had submerged her in the cosmic ocean.

Narasimha (The Man-Lion Avatar): Manifested as a half-man, half-lion to protect his devotee Prahlad and defeat the demon king Hiranyakashyap.

Vamana (The Dwarf Avatar): Took the form of a dwarf Brahmin to restore the universe from the demon king Bali, who was granted dominion over the three worlds by the gods.

Parashuram (The Warrior Sage Avatar): Incarnated as a Brahmin warrior to eliminate corrupt rulers and restore Dharma (righteousness) on Earth.

Lord Ram (The Prince of Ayodhya): Born in Ayodhya as Lord Ram, and showed everyone how to live a good and fair life. His life story is narrated in the epic Ramayana.

Lord Krishna (The Divine Cowherd): Considered the complete incarnation of Vishnu, Krishna's life and teachings are chronicled in the epic Mahabharata and the Bhagavad Gita.

Kalki (The Future Avatar): Foretold as the avatar yet to come, Kalki is believed to manifest at the end of the Kali Yuga (the current age of darkness and decline) to restore Dharma and bring a new era.

Each of these avatars of God Vishnu serves as a reminder of the importance of maintaining balance and righteousness in the universe, often appearing in times of turmoil or imbalance. They also serve as a symbol of hope and guidance for those who seek to live a life of dharma and uphold the principles of Hinduism.

Vishnu is also known and worshipped by several names. Some of his popular names are as follows:

Narayana: The Shelter or Refuge of All Beings.

Hari: The Remover of Sins.

Vasudeva: The Son of Vasudeva or the Dweller in All Beings.

Madhava: Consort of Ma (Goddess Lakshmi) and the Descendant of Madhu.

Vishnuvardhana: The Nourisher and Sustainer of the Universe.

Padmanabha: The Lotus-Naveled One.

Trivikrama: The Conqueror of the Three Worlds.

Jagannatha: God of the Universe.

Ananta: The Infinite One or the Endless.

Chakrapani: The Bearer of the Sudarshana Chakra (Discus).

As Devotees call upon these names in prayers, hymns, and rituals, they tap into specific energies embodied by each title, expressing reverence and seeking blessings from the divine on their journeys.

Chant Mantra of the Deity

Chant this mantra to honor God Vishnu, the sustainer of life and the guide to help you walk on the path of righteousness (dharma).

(Om Namo Narayana)

Meaning: "I bow to Narayana, the source of all beings."

Divine Form of the Deity

God Vishnu is often described as having a gentle blue complexion, with skin the color of a peaceful summer sky. He's portrayed with four arms, each holding a unique tool, whispering secrets about his role in our world.

Conch Shell (Shankha): The conch shell represents the call to awaken; when placed against our ear, we hear the ocean's roar. This sound embodies the essence of creation, the very echo of life that

Vishnu carries. It is meant to open our spirit and attune us to the symphony of existence.

Discus (Chakra): The spinning wheel blurring with speed, symbolizes the cyclical nature of life, the good and the bad, the ups and downs we all experience. It's also a guiding compass, symbolizing time's movement and the universal laws governing life and keeping everything balanced.

Lotus (Padma): The lotus flower emerges pristine from muddy water and embodies the beauty and resilience that Vishnu wants us to remember. The lotus symbolizes our souls, growing despite challenges and reaching for the light with inner strength and pure intentions.

Mace (Gada): The strong club symbolizes the power we have within ourselves to overcome any hurdle and stay on the right path even when things get tough.

The four arms show his vast powers, signifying his boundless reach and ability to care for every corner of the universe. Vishnu is known for his kindness, mercy, and willingness to guide us with gentleness and understanding as the caretaker of the cosmos.

Cultivating Connection

To deepen your devotion to God Vishnu, recite prayers and chants from sacred texts like the Bhagavad Gita and Vishnu Sahasranama. Focus on living in accordance with dharma, embracing your duties and responsibilities while cultivating positive karma through your actions. Strive to perform good deeds, act with integrity, and treat others with kindness. By aligning your life with the principles of dharma and committing to good karma, you will strengthen your connection with Vishnu and invite his divine presence into your daily experiences.

Om Namo Narayana

Lakshmi Devi - The Bestower of Wealth

Duty of the Deity

Goddess Lakshmi Devi is a highly-regarded deity in Hinduism, known for her role as the bestower of wealth, fortune, prosperity, and abundance. She is considered the consort of God Vishnu and is often depicted in Hindu art and mythology as a beautiful and benevolent goddess, showering blessings upon her devotees. In Hindu tradition, it is believed that worshipping Lakshmi Devi can bring good fortune and material success. She is mainly associated with acquiring wealth and financial prosperity. As such, she is often invoked by business owners, entrepreneurs, and individuals seeking economic stability and abundance in their lives.

Aspects of the Deity

Lakshmi is not only known for being Vishnu's consort but also has various manifestation forms (avatars) and is referred to by numerous names that depict different aspects of her divine nature and blessings. Each name and title describe different qualities of Lakshmi, highlighting her blessings and guidance in the pursuit of knowledge and wisdom.

Sita: Lakshmi incarnated as Sita, the consort of Lord Ram, in the epic Ramayana.

Rukmini: Another manifestation of Lakshmi, Rukmini is the principal wife of lord Krishna.

Padmavati: Worshiped as a form of Lakshmi in southern India.

Shri: A common prefix that invokes her, emphasizing her auspiciousness.

Padma: Padma, The Lotus symbolizes purity and beauty.

Kamala: Another name for Lakshmi, derived from the lotus (Kamal), representing beauty and grace.

Narayani: Consort of Narayana (God Vishnu).

Chanchala: The Playful One, emphasizing her elusive nature.

Vishnupriya: Beloved of Vishnu.

Haripriya: Dear to Hari (Vishnu).

Dhana Lakshmi: Goddess of Material Wealth.

Gaja Lakshmi: Associated with the well-being of elephants and represents abundance.

Adi Lakshmi: The Primordial Goddess of Wealth.

Aishwarya Lakshmi: Goddess of Prosperity and Opulence.

Vaibhav Lakshmi: Goddess of Wealth and Grandeur.

Each name and form of Goddess Lakshmi symbolizes a whole spectrum of prosperity, encompassing well-being, success, and a life filled with – auspiciousness.

Chant Mantra of the Deity

To honour Goddess Lakshmi, chant the following mantra and invite her divine energy into your life while cultivating gratitude and generosity.

(Om Shree Mahalakshmyai Namah)

Meaning: "I bow to the great goddess Lakshmi."

Divine Form of the Deity

Goddess Lakshmi, revered as the deity of wealth, prosperity, and fortune in Hinduism, is often depicted in a human-like form adorned with exquisite clothing. Her attire itself symbolizes the abundance and prosperity she represents. But her magic lies not just in her appearance – it's the stories her various attributes tell.

Her four arms signify aspects of humanity such as dharma/ righteousness, kama/desire, Artha/wealth, and Moksha/liberation from the life cycle.

The Lotus: Symbolizes purity, fertility, and enlightenment.

Abhaya Mudra (Gesture of Blessing): Symbolizes protection, fearlessness, and security assurance.

Varada Mudra (Gesture of Granting Wishes): Symbolizes granting blessings and wishes to her devotees.

Elephant: Often depicted beside her, the elephant symbolizes royalty, fertility, and auspiciousness.

Cascading Gold Coins: Perhaps the most iconic symbol associated with Lakshmi is the constant flow of gold coins cascading from her hands, symbolizing the continuous flow of wealth and prosperity that she bestows upon her devotees.

In simple terms, Goddess Lakshmi embodies everything we strive for – a life filled with prosperity, security, and the means to achieve our aspirations. Her human-like form makes her relatable, and her symbolic attributes remind us of the various dimensions of a truly fulfilling life. By inviting Lakshmi into our lives, we're not just asking for wealth; we seek wisdom and guidance to navigate a spiritually and materially prosperous life.

Cultivating Connection

The beauty of devotion lies in its simplicity, particularly in attracting wealth, prosperity, and abundance into your life. You create a sacred space that invites Lakshmi's blessings by chanting mantras, offering heartfelt prayers, and keeping a clean, welcoming home. Cultivate gratitude for your current blessings, recognizing that a thankful heart opens the door to greater prosperity. By consistently integrating these practices into your routine, you deepen your connection with Lakshmi, inviting her divine presence to guide you toward a life brimming with wealth, success, and fulfillment.

Om Shree Mahalakshmyai Namah

Shiva - The Transformer

Duty of the Deity

Shiva is one of the most important deities and is widely revered for his role as the destroyer and transformer within the Trimurti. His duty as a deity is to embody change and destruction, which paves the way for renewal and rejuvenation. This makes him a crucial figure in the cycle of life and death.

Aspects of the Deity

Shiva is also revered for his numerous manifestations, embodying different aspects of existence and cosmic principles. These prominent manifestations are known as Rudras or Forms and are revered by many Hindus.

Rudra (The Vedic Form): Rudra represents Shiva's raw power, often associated with storms and destruction. Think of him as the force of nature shaping the world in its primal state.

Mahadeva (The Great God): In contrast to Rudra's vedic form, Mahadeva radiates serenity and benevolence. He's the peaceful yogi, lost in meditation, reminding us of Shiva's inner peace and divine nature.

Nataraja (The Cosmic Dancer): This aspect of Shiva symbolizes the cosmic cycles of creation and destruction. Nataraja's dance is known as the Tandava. His every move represents the rhythm and flow of cosmic energy, reminding us of life's constant change.

Ardhanarishvara (The Androgynous Form): A powerful image of unity, Shiva, in this form, is half-man and half-woman, symbolizing the balance of masculine and feminine energies within us all. He reminds us that wholeness comes from embracing both sides.

Pashupatinath (The God of animals): With animals as his companions, Shiva as Pashupatinath signifies his connection with animals and nature, symbolizing his role as the protector of all living beings and reminding us of our responsibility to protect the natural world.

Bhairava (The Fierce Form): When evil needs vanquishing, Bhairava represents the ferocious aspect of Shiva, the formidable warrior. He is associated with the annihilation and destruction of evil forces.

Rishabh (The Ascetic Form): In this form, Shiva embodies the supreme ascetic, practicing deep meditation and detachment from worldly desires. He inspires us to seek inner peace and wisdom through mindful practices.

Dakshinamurthy (The Silent Guru): Seated in silence, Dakshinamurthy dispenses knowledge and wisdom not through words but through silent understanding. He reminds us that true learning often happens through contemplation and introspection.

Harihara (The Combined Form of Vishnu and Shiva): This form symbolizes the essential oneness and unity of all divine expressions. He reminds us that different paths lead to the same ultimate truth.

Karnataka (The Conqueror of Time): Shiva, in this form, stands tall, vanquishing even death and time. He offers hope and reminds us that our true essence transcends any physical limitations.

These manifestations highlight God Shiva's multifaceted nature, showcasing his roles as a peaceful yogi meditating on a mountaintop, a fierce warrior battling cosmic demons, a creator, a dancer, a teacher, and much more.

Shiva is revered by many names that highlight various aspects of his character, attributes, and cosmic roles.

Maheshwara/Mahadeva: These grand titles speak of his immense power and divinity.

Bholenath: This one hints at his playful and forgiving nature, like a Kind-hearted friend.

Shankara: The Auspicious One, bringing blessings and good fortune.

Neelakantha: The Blue-Throated One.

Trilochana: The Three-Eyed One symbolizes wisdom and insight.

Kailashpati: The God of Kailash (His celestial abode).

Girish: The God of the Mountains.

Kailashnath: The Ruler of Mount Kailash.

Mrityunjaya: The Conqueror of Death.

Veerabhadra: The Fearsome Warrior Form.

These names describe Shiva's different qualities and roles, giving us a glimpse into the vastness of the divine. Each name reflects a particular aspect of his character, helping people connect with and understand the divine better in their prayers and devotion.

Chant Mantra of the Deity

Chant this mantra to invoke Shiva, the path to spiritualization, meditation, and moksha.

(Om Namah Shivaya)

Meaning: "I bow to Shiva, the auspicious one."

Divine Form of the Deity

Shiva embodies deep spiritual meanings through his divine form. Each aspect of his form represents a unique spiritual lesson, encouraging individuals to strive toward spiritual liberation and a deeper understanding of the universe.

Third Eye (TriNetra): This represents inner vision, wisdom, and the ability to see beyond the apparent. It signifies enlightenment and the destruction of ignorance, urging individuals to look beyond the surface and embrace a deeper understanding of the world around them.

Matted Hair (Jata): This Symbolizes a free-spirited, untamed energy of life. It illustrates detachment from worldly desires and embraces the meditative state.

Crescent Moon (Chandra): Adorning his head, the crescent moon symbolizes time's eternal cycle and the rhythmic flow of life's phases. It encourages individuals to embrace life's cyclical nature and find comfort in the idea of impermanence.

Trident (Trishul): This symbol epitomizes cosmic power, embodying creation, preservation, and dissolution, showcasing the harmony of opposing forces.

Drum (Damaru): This represents the universal rhythm, the primal sound of creation, and the cosmic vibrations sustaining existence.

Snake (Naga): This Symbolizes the awakening of inner energy – (Kundalini) and transformation, shedding old limitations for spiritual growth. It encourages individuals to embrace change and transformation, shedding old habits and beliefs in favor of spiritual growth.

Ashes (Vibhuti): Wearing ashes signifies the transient nature of material existence. It emphasizes detachment and the impermanence of worldly attachments.

Ganges River (Ganga): The sacred river flowing from Shiva's locks symbolizes purity, spiritual purification, and divine grace. It encourages individuals to seek purity and spiritual cleansing, let go of negativity, and embrace the grace of the universe.

Each aspect of God Shiva's divine form embodies more profound spiritual lessons, encouraging detachment from the material world, embracing the cyclical nature of life, and awakening inner consciousness towards spiritual liberation.

Shiva and Shivling/Shivlingam

According to legend, a conflict arose between the Gods Brahma and Vishnu over their supremacy. To end their dispute, God Shiva appeared as a brilliant, never-ending light that spanned the universe like a cosmic pillar. This awe-inspiring form demonstrated that God Shiva was the most powerful, present everywhere and beyond all limits. The revelation of Shiva's supreme power and omnipresence taught Brahma and Vishnu valuable lessons, and their fight was stopped, emphasizing the importance of humility, resilience, collaboration, balance, and a deeper sense of purpose.

However, this form of light was too abstract for humans to comprehend and connect with. Therefore, Shiva transformed into the Shivling/ Shivlingam, a tangible form and sacred symbol, to make it easier for everyone to worship and feel closer to his divine presence. By worshipping the Shivling/ Shivlingam, we honor the formless aspect of Shiva, the Supreme Being.

Cultivating Connection

Practice mindfulness to connect with the tranquil essence of Shiva. Engage in meditation to immerse yourself in his teachings, allowing his profound wisdom to guide your spiritual journey. As the first yogi, Shiva is intrinsically linked to yoga; incorporating this sacred practice into your routine honors him. Dedicate time each day to meditate, focusing on your breath and envisioning Shiva's serene presence. Embrace transformation as a natural part of life, recognizing that endings and death pave the way for new beginnings.

Om Namah Shivaya

Adi Shakti Devi: Durga and Parvati

In the vast tapestry of Hinduism, one of the most captivating and multifaceted deities is the Divine Mother, Adi Shakti. Adi Shakti represents the primordial, supreme divine energy that is the source of all creation, power, and cosmic energy. Durga is the strong and protective manifestation or incarnation of this divine energy. Parvati, the divine consort of God Shiva, is the feminine power, love, and devotion of the manifestations or incarnations of this divine energy. They're like different sides of one divine goddess.

Duty of the Deity

The role of this deity is of a guardian, protecting everyone from harm and negativity. She stands for bravery and fairness, ensuring peace and goodness prevail over darkness.

Aspects of the Deity

Adi Shakti manifests in various avatars to maintain cosmic balance and protect creation. Each avatar embodies a specific quality or purpose, addressing the needs of the universe at a particular time.

Durga: Portrayed as a fierce warrior goddess. Dressed in radiant battle armor, mounted on a powerful lion, she embodies strength and courage to combat evil forces. With her ten arms wielding an arsenal of weapons, she is a force to be reckoned with.

Kali: Depicted in a fierce form, symbolizes the destruction of negativity, ego, and ignorance.

Mahakali: A more powerful and transcendent form of Kali, representing the ultimate reality.

Gauri: Emphasizes her fair complexion and purity, often associated with marital happiness.

Annapurna: Goddess of nourishment and food, symbolizing abundance and generosity.

Shakti: Represents divine feminine energy and creative power.

Parvati has other names and epithets that point towards the essence of the divine Feminine.

Uma: A name signifying beauty and grace.

Ambika: The Mother or the Divine Mother.

Haimavati: Daughter of the Majestic Himalayas, referring to her birthplace.

Aparna: One who abstained from food or penance, depicting her austerity.

Jagadamba: Mother of the universe.

Shivakamini: Beloved of God Shiva.

Shivakamalakshi: Consort of Shiva, the lotus-eyed goddess.

Whether through the fierce protection of Durga, the nurturing love of Parvati, or the raw power of Adi Shakti, the Divine Mother offers guidance, protection, and the boundless love that sustains creation. By understanding these various faces, we gain a deeper appreciation for the Divine Feminine's multifaceted nature and her profound role in our lives.

Chant Mantra of the Deity

(Hreem)

"Hreem" is a sacred bija (seed) sound that embodies the divine feminine energy. It is associated with Goddess Parvati, and when chanted, Hreem fosters love, strength, and creative power.

(Om Dum Durgaya Namah)

It translates to: " I bow to the divine Mother Durga." This chant expresses pure devotion. By reciting this mantra, you acknowledge Durga's powerful presence and seek her guidance and protection.

Divine Form of the Deity

The goddess is often shown typically with eight to ten arms, each holding a distinct object imbued with symbolic meaning.

Conch Shell (Shankha): Representing spiritual victory and awakening.

Discus (Chakra): Representing time's movement and cosmic law.

Lotus (Padma): Representing purity and spiritual growth.

Bow and Arrow: Representing focus and determination.

Trident (Trishul): Showing control over creation and balance.

Sword: Representing strength and knowledge to overcome obstacles.

Mace (Gada): Showing power to defeat negativity.

Shield: Symbolizing protection against evil, keeping her devotees safe.

These powerful objects in Durga's hands are a visual testament to her strength, determination, and unwavering commitment to fight evil for the greater good and the safety of her followers.

Cultivating Connection

Embodying the loving spirit of Durga requires a heartfelt commitment to integrating her essence into your daily life. Begin each day with sincere devotion, expressing love and gratitude to forge a deep connection with her divine energy. As the Divine Mother and protector, Durga lovingly answers those who seek her guidance. Channel her fearless courage to confront injustice while nurturing the inner strength to embrace life's challenges with grace. Reflect her compassion through gentle acts of kindness and draw inspiration from her legendary battles to face adversity with resilience. Remain open to receiving her blessings of strength, courage, and the loving resolve to conquer any obstacle in your path.

Om Dum Durgaya Namah

ॐ

Ganesh - Remover of Obstacles

Duty of the Deity

Ganesh, God Shiva's Son, is responsible for removing all obstacles from life and clearing the way for progress. Hindus traditionally invoke Ganesh before undertaking any new endeavor, seeking his blessings to overcome potential roadblocks and ensure a successful outcome. His presence symbolizes the removal of negativity, self-doubt, and external challenges that might hinder your goals.

Aspects of the Deity

Ganesh, the beloved elephant-headed deity in Hinduism, holds a place of immense love and respect. He is worshipped for his wisdom, intellect, and ability to remove obstacles, paving the way for a smooth and successful journey in life. While Ganesh is predominantly worshipped in his familiar form, a few other manifestations and names are associated with him.

Mahaganapati: Depicted with multiple arms and attributes, symbolizing his great power and authority.

Dhumraketu: A rare form of Ganesh, depicting his smoky or dark complexion.

Bhalchandra: Refers to the moon-shaped mark on his forehead, resembling a crescent moon.

Vinayaka: A popular name for Ganesh, signifying the leader or guide of the divine forces.

Vighnaharta: Symbolizing the Remover of Obstacles.

Gajanana: Meaning the Elephant-Faced One.

Ekadanta: One with a single tusk, representing his strength and determination.

Lambodara: The one with a potbelly symbolizing prosperity and the ability to digest both good and bad experiences in life.

Ganapati: Symbolizing the leader of the Ganas (celestial beings).

Heramba: Symbolizing the Protector of the Weak or the Compassionate One.

Siddhidata: Meaning the Bestower of Success and Accomplishment.

These names and manifestations of Lord Ganesh depict different aspects of his divine attributes, symbolism, and qualities. His endearing elephant head is a constant reminder of his wisdom and gentleness, while his potbelly symbolizes his ability to absorb and overcome all obstacles. For Hindus and anyone seeking a benevolent guiding force, Ganesh remains a beloved deity, revered for his ability to clear the path for a fulfilling and successful journey.

Chant Mantra of the Deity

Chant this mantra to remove any obstacles you may be facing in your life. It is traditionally recited before making a purchase or starting any new endeavor to ensure a smooth journey ahead.

(Om Gam Ganapataye Namah)

Meaning: "I bow to Ganesh, the remover of obstacles."

Divine Form of the Deity

Lord Ganesh, a beloved deity in Hinduism, embodies profound spirituality and holistic symbolism through his entire divine form, enriching our spiritual understanding and connection.

Elephant Head: This symbolizes profound wisdom, intelligence, and a higher understanding of life's mysteries. It is a constant inspiration, reminding us that the path to enlightenment requires a deep understanding of ourselves and the world around us. This wisdom isn't simply knowledge; it's the ability to see through the illusions and grasp the true essence of life.

Large Ears: His large ears signify the importance of listening not just to the world around us but also to our inner voice and our intuition. Ganesh encourages us to be patient and truly listen, for it's within that space that true growth and inspiration can be found.

Small Eyes: Ganesh's small eyes, a paradox in themselves, hold a profound message. They symbolize focused perception, the ability to see beyond the ordinary and perceive the divine in all things. Ganesh urges us to cultivate this focused gaze, to see the good, bad, and extraordinary in every experience.

Trunk: His trunk Reflects adaptability and navigating life's twists and turns. More importantly, it symbolizes the strength and determination to clear obstacles on the spiritual journey. These obstacles can be external challenges, hardships, and setbacks but also internal doubts, fears, and negative thoughts.

Tusk: Ganesh's broken tusk is a powerful symbol of sacrifice for a greater purpose and a testament to spiritual dedication.

Large Stomach: Ganesh's large stomach symbolizes the capacity to embrace life's experiences, digesting both the sweet and bitter with equanimity.

Four Arms: Each arm holds spiritual tools - the ability to cut attachments, capture desires, embrace sacrifice, and attain spiritual fulfillment.

Mouse as Vehicle: Choosing a modest mouse as a vehicle signifies humility. While most deities choose powerful animals as companions, Ganesh chooses a small rodent. This signifies the importance of humility on the path to spiritual elevation.

Ganesh's divine form serves as a spiritual guide, teaching profound lessons of wisdom, humility and the journey toward transcending obstacles on the path to spiritual enlightenment.

Cultivating Connection

Express your devotion through prayer, seeking guidance and wisdom from Ganesh, the remover of obstacles. Begin new endeavors by invoking Ganesh's blessings first. Embrace challenges with resilience and a positive spirit, embodying Ganesh's symbolism of overcoming difficulties. By weaving these practices into your daily routine, you deepen your spiritual connection with Lord Ganesh, gaining strength, wisdom, and unwavering support on your path to spiritual fulfillment.

Om Gam Ganapataye Namah

Lord Ram/Rama

Duty of the Deity

Rama, a name synonymous with virtue and righteousness, is a central figure in Hinduism. He's not just an incarnation of God Vishnu but an embodiment of the ideal human being who upheld his duty (dharma) even in the face of immense difficulty.

Aspects of the Deity

The story of Lord Ram is intricately linked to another prominent Hindu deity, Vishnu. According to legend, the world became terrifying, ruled by the demon king Ravan, who revelled in evil. Vishnu chose to descend to earth in human form as Lord Ram to restore balance and vanquish this darkness. This divine intervention signifies the importance of good overcoming evil, a theme that resonates across different cultures and religions.

Chant Mantra of the Deity

Chant this Mantra to invoke and connect with Lord Ram.

(Om Shri Ramaya Namah)

Meaning: "I bow to Rama, the embodiment of virtue."

Divine Form of the Deity

Rama, a revered deity in Hinduism, is depicted in a human form with significant attributes.

The Brave Warrior: Often depicted with a bow and arrow, Rama represents strength and courage. He symbolizes the importance of – standing up for what is right, even when difficult.

The Divine Aura: A slight blue tinge in some depictions signifies his divine nature. It's a subtle reminder that Lord Ram possesses a celestial essence while he walks among humans.

Royal Lineage: The elegant crown adorning Lord Ram's head signifies his royal ancestry. He is a model leader who demonstrates responsibility and compassion towards his people.

In essence, Lord Ram embodies righteousness, integrity, and courage. He inspires us to integrate these values into our lives. He sets a standard for honorable leadership, courageous action, and unwavering commitment to family.

Cultivating Connection

Read the Ramayana, a Hindu epic, to gain deeper insights into Lord Ram's virtues and the lessons he imparts. Seek strength and guidance through prayer, and face challenges with the grace and resilience embodied by Lord Ram. Strive to do what is right, following the path of dharma. Incorporate these values into daily life to build a strong and special connection with the revered Lord Ram.

Om Shri Ramaya Namah

Lord Krishna

Krishna, a name that resonates throughout Hinduism, is more than just a deity. He's a multifaceted personality, a wise counsellor, a mischievous child, and a symbol of unwavering devotion. Considered an avatar, or incarnation, of the God Vishnu, Krishna descended to Earth to restore balance and guide humanity towards righteousness.

Duty of the Deity

Krishna is a manifestation of God Vishnu. Through the Bhagavad Gita, a holy scripture embedded within the Mahabharata, Krishna guides Prince Arjuna during a crucial war, teaching the importance of fulfilling one's duty (dharma) without succumbing to crippling anxieties about the outcome. This message of karma yoga, the path of selfless action, transcends the battlefield and becomes a core principle for a balanced life. Krishna teaches us to do our best, act with integrity, and detach ourselves from the fruits of our actions.

Aspects of the Deity

Krishna's life and teachings, chronicled in the epic Mahabharata, particularly the Bhagavad Gita, inspire and influence millions today. Krishna is known for his multifaceted persona and various roles.

Vishnu's Incarnation: Hindus believe that Vishnu, the preserver god, descends to Earth when balance is needed to uphold dharma. Krishna is considered one of these incarnations. His arrival on Earth signifies a time of renewal and hope for humanity.

Balakrishna: The childhood form of Krishna, often depicted with blue skin and adorned with feathers, this endearing portrayal highlights Krishna's innocent charm and his ability to bring joy.

Govinda: Govinda translates to "protector of cows." Cows are considered sacred animals in Hinduism. This title signifies Krishna's association with pastoral life, his role as a cowherd during his youth, and his deep connection to nature. Govinda also embodies the aspect of Krishna that brings joy to the senses.

Gopala: Gopala refers explicitly to Krishna's time spent in Vrindavan, a region associated with his childhood and youthful pastimes.

Murlidhar: The one who holds the divine flute.

Hari: Signifying the remover of sorrows.

Nandalal: Son of Nanda (his foster father), reflecting his familial ties in Vrindavan.

Yashoda Nandan: The beloved son of Yashoda, his foster mother.

Madhava: Referring to Krishna's association with the sweetness of his actions and character.

Kanhaiya: A popular name in North India, Kanhaiya is often used to describe the playful and mischievous aspects of Krishna's childhood.

Dwarkadheesh: The ruler or king of Dwarka, where Krishna established his kingdom.

Krishna is celebrated and worshipped for his teachings on righteousness, love, duty, and devotion. Krishna's story inspires millions of devotees worldwide, from his playful childhood pranks in Vrindavan to his pivotal role in the epic Mahabharata. Devotees invoke the various names of Krishna in prayers, bhajans (devotional songs), and rituals to seek his blessings for spiritual growth, prosperity, and guidance in life's journey.

Chant Mantra of the Deity

Invoke Lord Krishna's divine presence with the following mantra.

(Hare Krishna, Hare Krishna, Krishna Krishna, Hare Hare; Hare Rama, Hare Rama, Rama Rama Hare Hare)

Meaning: This chant invokes Lord Krishna and Rama's names for spiritual connection, grace, and inner peace.

Divine Form of the Deity

Krishna, a beloved deity in Hinduism, is portrayed in a human form with key attributes.

Youthful Appearance: Krishna is depicted as a charming and youthful figure, often with a peacock feather adorning his hair.

Flute: He's often seen playing a flute, symbolizing harmony, love, and divine music that captivates hearts. It's the melody of love, devotion, and the call to connect with the divine.

Blue Complexion: His blue skin represents depth, divinity, and infinity, signifying the vastness of the universe.

Peacock Feather: Adorning Krishna's crown, it represents beauty, grace, and Krishna's connection to nature.

Cows: Depicted with cows, symbolizing simplicity, purity, and the pastoral environment of his childhood.

In simple terms, Lord Krishna embodies love, joy, and divinity. His human-like form and endearing attributes signify his teachings on love, righteousness, and pursuing spirituality through devotion and wisdom.

Cultivating Connection

To feel a connection with Krishna, seek guidance through prayers, embodying Krishna's compassionate spirit. Extend kindness and understanding to others, reflecting Krishna's teachings on harmony.

Additionally, explore the sacred Hindu scripture, the Bhagavad Gita, where Krishna imparts profound wisdom on duty and spiritual realization. Apply these lessons in your life, integrating the timeless wisdom of the Gita into your daily decisions.

Hare Krishna, Hare Krishna, Krishna Krishna, Hare Hare; Hare Rama, Hare Rama, Rama Rama Hare Hare

Lord Hanuman

Hanuman, the monkey god, is a beloved figure in Hinduism. He is revered for his unwavering devotion, immense strength, and unwavering loyalty. His story, intricately woven into the epic Ramayana, continues to inspire millions across the globe.

Duty of the Deity

Hanuman's primary purpose was to serve and assist Lord Ram, the incarnation of God Vishnu, on Earth. When Lord Ram's wife, Sita, was abducted by the demon king Ravan, Hanuman stepped forward as a champion of duty. He embarked on a perilous journey to Lanka, Ravan's island kingdom, to find Sita and deliver a message from Lord Ram.

Hanuman's bravery and resourcefulness are legendary. He infiltrated Lanka, disguised as a tiny monkey, and found Sita imprisoned in a grove. He reassured her of Lord Ram's unwavering determination to rescue her and, as a defiant act, burned down a significant part of Lanka before making his escape. This act demoralized Ravan's forces and served as a powerful symbol of Hanuman's unwavering devotion to Lord Ram's cause. Hanuman inspires us to face challenges bravely, stay devoted, and be loyal. His courage teaches us to confront our fears; his devotion shows the power of dedication, and his loyalty reminds us to support our loved ones and values.

Aspects of the Deity

In Hinduism, Hanuman embodies the essence of Rudra, an aspect of God Shiva's representation of energies. Hanuman is primarily revered for his devotion to Lord Ram, an incarnation of God Vishnu, rather than being known as a direct Rudra form of Shiva.

Chant Mantra of the Deity

Om Hum Hanumate Namah

Meaning: "I bow to Hanuman."

Divine Form of the Deity

Hanuman, a revered figure in Hinduism, is depicted in a human-like form with significant attributes.

Monkey-Like Appearance: Hanuman is often depicted with a monkey face and a muscular body.

Orange Colored Body: His color symbolizes courage, bravery, and devotion.

Mace (Gada): Often shown carrying a mace, symbolizing strength, power, and the ability to overcome obstacles.

Tail: Sometimes depicted with a long tail, emphasizing his monkey form and agility.

Mountains on Hand: In some depictions, Hanuman carries mountains, representing his immense strength and power.

Hanuman embodies unwavering devotion, strength, and selfless service. His human-like attributes symbolize dedication, loyalty, and the embodiment of a true devotee in the Hindu belief system.

Cultivating Connection

The most popular way to connect with Hanuman is by reciting the Hanuman Chalisa and Bajrang Ban among devotees to connect with Hanuman's protective and powerful spirit. Embrace qualities such as loyalty, devotion, and humility, mirroring the ideals upheld by Hanuman. By incorporating these practices, you deepen your connection with him and draw on his virtues to navigate the challenges of your own life.

Om Hum Hanumate Namah

Directions and Elements in Hinduism

In Hinduism, the world around us isn't just a backdrop for human existence. It's a vibrant tapestry woven from divine threads, where every direction and element are seen as special and respected, almost like they're special guardians representing divine powers or gods.

Directions

In Hinduism, the directions are not just geographical points but sacred pathways with a celestial guardian or deity watching over them. Devotees pay homage to the guardians of different directions, reciting prayers or mantras specific to each direction during worship ceremonies. These guardians, often called Lokapalas, are powerful deities who ensure order and balance in their respective domains.

Indra, the Lord of the East: The rising sun paints the eastern sky, symbolizing new beginnings and hope. Here reigns Indra, the king of the gods, wielding his mighty thunderbolt to ward off evil and ensure prosperity.

Agni, the Fiery Guardian of the South: The South is associated with fire, the element of transformation and purification. Agni, the fire god, resides here, consuming impurities and offering warmth and light. Agni also serves as the divine messenger, carrying offerings to the gods during rituals and sacrifices.

Yama, the Lord of the South: Yama, also governing the South, represents the dual aspects of cosmic balance: Yama governs the realm of the dead and oversees the justice of souls' journeys in the afterlife, while Agni embodies transformation and purification through fire. Together, they symbolize the interconnectedness of endings and renewal in the cycle of existence.

Nirriti, the Guardian of the Southwest: In the southwest, where the sun sets, resides Nirriti, the guardian deity. Often depicted with a dark complexion and wielding a sword, she symbolizes the destructive aspects of nature and the importance of balance. Despite her fierce appearance, Nirriti is also a protector, ensuring that endings pave the way for new beginnings.

Varuna, the Water God of the West: As the sun dips below the horizon in the west, ushering in darkness, we encounter Varuna, the God of water. Water represents purification and sustenance, essential for all life. Water offering during Puja is a way to honor Varuna's life-giving power.

Vayu, the Guardian of the Northwest: In the northwest, where the winds blow, Vayu, the God of wind, holds sway. Often depicted as a powerful deity riding the clouds, he symbolizes movement, change, and the unseen forces of nature. Vayu brings freshness and vitality, stirring the air and clearing stagnant energies.

Kubera, the Guardian of Wealth in the North: The north, the direction of the North Star, symbolizes stability and immovable foundations. Kubera, the lord of wealth, presides over this domain, ensuring prosperity and material well-being.

Ishana, the Guardian of the Northeast: In the northeast, where new beginnings take root, Ishana, a form of God Shiva, presides. As a serene figure with a third eye, he embodies purity, transformation, and enlightenment. Ishana's energy is gentle yet powerful, inspiring growth and spiritual evolution.

Additionally, two more celestial guardians cover the zenith (the sky above) and nadir (the ground below), bringing the total to ten Guardians.

Elements (Pancha Bhoota)

Hinduism believes the world has five elements: Earth, Water, Fire, Air, and Space (Akash). Each element is imbued with its unique energy and is presided over by a powerful deity.

The Rig Veda has also emphasized the importance of Panch Tatva (the five elements): Prithivi (earth), Pavan (air), Jal (water), Tej (solar energy), and Nabh (sky). It is said that the entire life system on Earth is based on the harmonious functioning of these five elements.

Prithvi (Earth): The solid foundation of our existence, Earth is revered for its nurturing and grounding energy. Goddess Bhumi Devi, the Earth Mother, is associated with this element. Offerings of flowers or fruits during Puja can be a way to express gratitude for the Earth's bounty.

Jal (Water): Life cannot exist without water, the element of purification and flow. Varuna, the God we encountered as the guardian of the West, also embodies the divine essence of water. During rituals, sprinkling water can symbolize cleansing and the flow of life force.

Agni (Fire): Fire can be destructive but also transformative. The fire god Agni embodies this duality, consuming impurities and bringing illumination. Lighting lamps during Puja is a way to honor Agni's purifying power.

Vayu (Air): The breath of life, the ever-present yet invisible force that's Vayu, the air god. He represents movement, communication, and the life force that sustains all living beings. Pranayama (yogic breathing exercises) is a way to connect with Vayu's energy.

Akash (Space): Beyond the tangible elements lies Akash, the all-encompassing space that holds everything within it. It represents the vastness of the universe, the source of all creation. Meditation practices often involve focusing on the vastness within ourselves, reflecting the limitless Akash.

Devotion of Celestial Bodies

Hindus honor celestial bodies like the Sun (Surya) and the Moon (Chandra) through rituals and practices that reflect their deep spiritual importance. These rituals include offerings, meditations, and observances recognizing these celestial entities' divine qualities and cosmic significance in Hindu tradition.

Surya (Sun)

Surya, the Sun God, symbolizes light, energy, and consciousness. Surya gives life-giving energy, embodying the cosmic order. Its energy sustains life on Earth, regulates seasons, and is integral to agricultural cycles. Rituals like offering water to the Sun at sunrise show reverence and gratitude for its role in sustaining life. In yoga, Sun salutations (Surya Namaskar) energize the body and honor the Sun's spiritual significance, connecting practitioners to its physical and metaphysical aspects and seeking blessings for health, prosperity, and spiritual awakening.

Chandra (Moon)

Chandra, the Moon God, is revered for his calming influence and symbolic representation of the mind. Devotees perform rituals and meditative practices during the full moon (Purnima) and the new moon (Amavasya) phases to enhance mental clarity and emotional balance. In yoga, Chandra Namaskar (Moon salutations) harness lunar energies for spiritual growth. Chandra's worship emphasizes emotional stability and introspection, which are essential for spiritual enlightenment in Hindu traditions.

Devotion of the Directions and Elements

Devotion to the directions and elements in Hinduism is expressed through the harmonious integration of rituals and pujas for specific deities associated with each direction or element. Aligning living spaces with the cardinal directions and Vastu Shastra, an ancient Indian science similar to Feng Shui, helps balance elemental energies and fosters a deeper connection. Vedic practices like Havan and ceremonial offerings to nature express this reverence. Mindful living, such as conserving resources and reducing environmental impact, is a tangible manifestation of devotion.

Chapter 3

Puja 101

Complete Step-by-Step Guide

Throughout my journey, I've discovered the immense depth and significance behind Puja rituals. This chapter is my attempt to share that journey with you, offering insights, step-by-step instructions, and the essence of Puja. Whether you're new to these practices or seeking a deeper understanding, I hope that this chapter will help you embrace and cherish the spiritual richness Puja brings into your life.

Understanding Puja

What is Puja

In Hindu traditions, Puja is deeply significant as a sacred ritual that fosters a profound connection with the divine. It's more than just a set of actions; it's a heartfelt communion with the spiritual realm. Imagine Puja as a serene conversation with the divine, where individuals express gratitude, seek blessings, and nurture their spiritual bond. It's a beautiful way to honor and acknowledge the presence of the divine forces that shape our lives.

It's an act of offering our love and respect to the various manifestations of the divine, be it a deity, a formless energy, or the universe itself. Rituals, prayers, and offerings remind us of our interconnectedness with the spiritual realm and the larger cosmos.

What is the Purpose of Puja

In Hindu traditions, puja serves multiple purposes. First, it acts as a bridge between the individual and the divine, providing a space for personal and spiritual growth.

Second, Puja expresses gratitude and seeks blessings for various aspects of life, health, prosperity, success, or familial well-being. It's a way of seeking guidance, wisdom, and strength from the divine forces.

Furthermore, Puja plays a significant role in fostering a sense of community and cultural continuity. It's not just an individual practice but often a communal one, where families or communities come together to celebrate festivals, perform rituals, and partake in the shared heritage and traditions, strengthening the bond of unity.

Importantly, Puja isn't confined to a rigid set of rules. It's a flexible practice that can be personalized based on individual beliefs and preferences. It encourages introspection, spiritual practices like meditation and mantra chanting, and the study of sacred texts to deepen one's spiritual understanding.

Overall, Puja reminds us that there's something divine in our lives, making us appreciate and respect the immense and mysterious universe.

Puja in Temples and Homes

In Hinduism, temples are revered as the sacred homes of deities, serving as earthly dwellings where the divine presence resides. Here, the Pujari, or priest, takes on the caretaker role, ensuring the well-being of the deities and their sanctuary. When a new deity statue arrives, Pujaris conduct the prana pratishtha, a profound ritual that infuses the idols with divine life force through sacred chants and offerings. This transformative process imbues the idol with spiritual significance, elevating it from a mere statue to a living representation of the deity.

Pujaris meticulously attend to the deities' needs, performing bathing, feeding, and praying rituals. Pujaris are the caretakers of the living gods in temples, where devotees are welcomed as guests. When visiting temples, devotees offer bhog (food) and other offerings to the gods, which Pujaris receive on their behalf. In return, devotees receive prasad and charnamrit as blessings from the gods, symbolizing a sacred exchange of devotion and hospitality. This profound connection between devotees, Pujaris, and the divine fosters a deep reverence and spiritual fulfillment in the temple environment.

Visiting temples holds immense significance. It allows devotees to connect with the divine in a sacred space. Temples serve as sanctuaries where individuals can offer prayers, seek blessings, and find solace amidst the hustle and bustle of daily life.

Having a Temple at home and bringing deity idols at home requires sincerity, devotion, and adherence to tradition. Devotees can prepare a sacred space or altar for their home idols and invite the deity's presence into their home through their heartfelt intentions. As the deity is considered to be living within the home, it becomes important to take care of them. Ensuring your home is clean and serene sets a fitting atmosphere for their presence. Additionally, maintaining a regular schedule of Puja and offering food, flowers, and water daily is essential in nurturing the spiritual bond and fostering a sense of devotion and reverence within the household.

Setting Up a Puja Temple (Mandir)

Setting up a Hindu temple (Mandir) or a sacred space at home involves creating a dedicated area for worship and spiritual practices. Here are some simple steps to consider when setting up a Hindu temple at home.

Create a Sacred Haven

Discover a serene, well-ventilated space within your home that speaks to your inner calmness. This can be a room dedicated to tranquillity or a particular corner where you can connect with your spirituality and engage in moments of reflection and reverence. According to our Hindu books and studies, the northeast is believed to be the ideal direction because it helps imbue the maximum solar energy.

Embrace Divine Presence

Choose an idol or an image embodying the divine presence you wish to honor. It could be representations of various deities, like a formless representation of Shiva in the form of a Shivling or idols and images of Ganesh, Shiva, Lakshmi, Durga, Krishna, or any other deity close to your heart. Through heartfelt intentions, invite the deity's presence into the home, becoming caretakers of them and their sacred place of living, the home temple.

Elevate the Altar

With utmost respect, position the idol or image in the east direction for worship on an elevated platform adorned with cleanliness and care. Adorn the altar with the sacred symbols that resonate with your spirituality.

Gather Ritual Tools/Elements

Arrange essential elements for worship, including fragrant incense sticks or dhoop, illuminating oil (diyas) or candles, a gentle bell, Tika or Tilak, Moli thread, and a Puja Thali (tray) for offerings.

Prepare Offerings and Ritual Essentials

Prepare offerings such as fresh fruits, fragrant flowers, coconut, sweets, sugar, and any other items revered by the deity you worship. Keep a plate or bowl for distributing prasad.

Create a Sacred Seat

Prepare your seat in front of the temple with a mat, a clean sheet, or a cushion underneath you rather than directly on the floor.

Maintain Cleanliness

Uphold the sanctity of the sacred space by diligently maintaining its cleanliness. Regular dusting and tidying ensure a serene and unpolluted environment, upholding spiritual purity.

Engage in daily Devotions (Puja)

Establish a ritualistic routine for daily worship. This may encompass lighting incense, presenting flowers, reciting prayers, performing Arti, and offering bhog (food) to the deity. As the caretaker of their temple within your home, attending to their needs becomes paramount. Ensuring your home is clean and serene sets a fitting atmosphere for their presence. Additionally, maintaining a regular schedule of Puja is essential in nurturing the spiritual bond and fostering a sense of devotion and reverence within the household.

Celebrate Festivals and Special Moments

Celebrate auspicious festivals and special occasions by embellishing the sacred space, conducting elaborate ceremonies, and offering heartfelt prayers and delicacies to the deity.

Embrace Spiritual Practices

Beyond rituals, embrace spiritual disciplines such as meditation, chanting, studying sacred scriptures, and self-reflection within this consecrated space to deepen your spiritual connection.

Honor Sacred Space

Cultivate a reverential attitude towards the sacred area. Avoid placing footwear or positioning yourself in ways that detract from the sanctity of the space. Infuse every action with respect and veneration for this holiness.

In the end, putting up a Puja temple or altar entails a sequence of simple yet significant steps. The selection of a holy place, the arrangement of essential items, and the devotional performance of the rituals transform the space into one that enables spiritual connection. Following these steps makes the temple a place of worship, meditation, and good vibes where everyone can have a spiritual experience.

Using Symbols & Sacred Items

Certain symbols, tools, and items hold profound significance in Puja as gateways to deeper spiritual connections. Let's delve into their essence and spiritual meaning to understand their role in enhancing the divine atmosphere during Puja.

OM/ AUM ॐ

"Om," also spelled "Aum," is a sacred sound and a spiritual icon in Hinduism. It represents the essence of the ultimate reality, consciousness, or Atman (soul). The sound of "Om" is considered the sound of the universe, encompassing all that is, was, and will be.

Breaking down "Om"

A - Brahma: The sound "A" is linked to Brahma, the creator deity. It signifies the beginning, birth, and the creative aspect of the divine.

U - Vishnu: The sound "U" is associated with Vishnu, the preserver deity. It represents continuity, preservation, and the sustaining force in the universe.

M - Shiva: The sound "M" is connected to Shiva, the destroyer deity. It symbolizes dissolution, destruction, and the transformative aspect of the divine.

The complete sound, "Aum," thus encompasses the trinity of creation, preservation, and destruction embodied by Brahma, Vishnu, and Shiva. Chanting "Aum" is a way to invoke the essence of the Trideva Gods and align oneself with the cosmic forces governing the universe in Hindu belief. "Om" is often said at the beginning and end of prayers, mantras, and meditation sessions in Hinduism.

Swastika 卐

Swastika holds special significance in Hindu tradition for Pujas and is derived from three Sanskrit roots: Su, meaning 'good'; Asti, meaning 'exists, there is, or to be'; and Ka, meaning 'make.' Combined, they translate to the 'making of goodness,' interpreted as the marker of good luck and auspiciousness.

The Swastika, with its four arms and distinctive lines, symbolizes the four cardinal directions and the balance of cosmic forces, reflecting the cyclical nature of the universe. Linked to the sun and divine light, it represents enlightenment and dispelling of ignorance. Additionally, the swastika embodies the principle of dharma, or righteousness, and invokes divine blessings and protection.

Engaging in the ritual of drawing it with your right ring finger in a clockwise direction before a Puja, using red powders like Tilak, Kumkum, or Tika, is a significant practice. This tradition is rooted in the belief that the Swastika fuses positive energy and divine power, dispelling negativity and inviting blessings.

When placed at the beginning of essential activities, ceremonies, festivals, and Pujas, the Swastika attracts positive vibes. Much like the practice of worshiping Ganesh before any other deity, it contributes to making the Puja space feel divinely special.

When drawing the Swastika, remember that its center, arms, and bent arms carry significant symbolic meanings. To honor their traditional significance with care and respect, it's essential to follow strict guidelines. Whether you follow step-by-step instructions, purchase a symbol, or opt for a readymade one, drawing the Swastika with mindfulness adds a beautiful touch to your Puja.

Tilak/Tika

Tika is a mark applied to the forehead commonly seen in Hindu Pujas, rituals, and ceremonies. It holds cultural and religious significance, symbolizing blessings and auspiciousness.

The spot on the forehead where tilak goes is the place of the 3rd eye center, the place of Ājñā Chakra. Applying tilak, or tika activates the sacredness of the third eye center.

For men, tilak is usually applied with the thumb in a vertical or u-shaped symbol, showing fire and powerful energy. For women, tilak is applied with the ring finger, showing the feminine and gentle energy of the moon, making a dot or bindi.

Some spiritual people also apply tilak on their other body parts, such as the throat to activate their throat chakras, the heart area to activate the heart chakra, and the belly to activate the Solar Chakra.

Another part of this tradition is putting unbroken rice grains on the tilak. This makes the ritual complete, infusing it with positive energy. Rice is a symbol of abundance and fertility. This gesture is more than a mark on the forehead to invoke blessings of prosperity and divine energy.

Holy Ash

Vibhuti, also known as Bhasma or Holy Ash, is a sacred substance made from burnt wood, cow dung, and rice husk. If Vibhuti is unavailable, clay or ash from hawan and other spiritual fire ceremonies can be used. Applied to the forehead during rituals, Vibhuti symbolizes purification and divine blessings. Devotees of Shiva often mark the Tripundra, or three horizontal lines, on their foreheads with Vibhuti, signifying that the body is merely a vessel and not the essence. The Tripundra represents the three powers of human intention—Kriya Shakti (action), Iccha Shakti (will), and Gyana Shakti (knowledge)—corresponding to the forms of Shiva. This symbol also reflects the divine stages of creation, sustenance, and destruction, embodying the unity of energy and matter. Applying the Tripundra is believed to cleanse one of the sins from this and past lives.

Traditionally, Vibhuti is applied with the ring and middle fingers on the forehead. Two lines are drawn horizontally from left to right; a third line is drawn beneath these two lines with the index finger. Finally, a sandalwood dot is applied in the center of these lines with the middle finger. Vibhuti, like tika, can also be applied to the throat, chest, or other body parts.

Moli/Sacred Thread

Moli, a thread used in Hindu ceremonies and worn on the wrist, derives its name from the Sanskrit word "Mauli," meaning 'sacred thread. The moli thread is a symbol of protection, a shield against negativity. It is tied during Pujas, weddings, and other auspicious occasions, mostly on the right hand for males and the left hand for females. The right side, often associated with men, embodies strength and stillness, akin to the qualities of God Shiva. On the -left side, linked with women, it signifies creativity and dynamic energy, reminiscent of Goddess Parvati. This practice symbolizes a beautiful balance of energies in our lives, much like Ardhanarishvara, a special form of God Shiva displaying half man on the right and half woman on the left.

Beyond tradition, there's a fascinating scientific perspective. Wearing the moli on the wrist subtly impacts acupressure points, positively influencing the body's energy flow. The moli is typically worn for 3 weeks before it is ceremoniously removed and disposed of, often by tying it to a tree or burying it beneath a tree or plant.

Conch Shell (Shankh)

The conch shell is a special symbol in Hinduism, often seen in ceremonies like Puja. People use it to purify the space and invite the divine during worship. The conch is like a spiritual trumpet, making a unique sound believed to be powerful and pure. Blowing the conch shell during Hindu ceremonies sends a sacred invitation to the divine that we're starting something important, and we'd love your blessings. People believe the conch shell sound awakens our spiritual side and helps us feel closer to the divine.

Ghanti/Bell

"Ghanti" is the Hindi word for bell. It is used in prayers and Pujas to invoke the divine and signify the beginning and end of worship. The sacred resonance of the Puja bell, or ghanti, carries a profound message to the divine. Each gentle ring beckons the presence of higher energies, signalling the initiation of spiritual connection. The bell invokes divine blessings and creates a space where the earthly and spiritual realms intertwine. The ringing of the ghanti is believed to purify the surroundings, dispel negative energies, and focus the minds of worshippers on the sacred moment.

Puja Diya/Lamp

The Puja diya, crafted from Flour dough, clay, or metal, is a radiant beacon in Hindu ceremonies. Before lighting it, we carefully clean and fill it with mustard oil or ghee, creating a pure space and symbolically welcoming positive knowledge.

Each part of the diya holds meaning –The material, whether clay or metal, connects the spiritual and earthly. Oil or ghee represents purity and surrender to the divine, making the space sacred. The wick is like our soul, soaking up knowledge for enlightenment. We combine these meaningful parts by lighting the Puja Diya, creating a connection with the divine. Lighting the diya symbolically means moving from darkness to light.

In Hindu Pujas or traditions, circling a diya/lamp around the deity called Arti symbolizes the cyclic nature of life. The Clockwise direction of circling the lamp during Puja symbolizes respect, devotion, and a harmonious connection with the divine. This direction is believed to follow the sun's path and is a progression emphasizing a sense of order and positive alignment with cosmic energies during ceremonies.

Things to consider while lighting Diya

- Diya shall be lit with an intention.
- Diya shall be placed on a plate with rice or wheat for respect and to bring in the auspicious energy.
- Diya shall be placed on the Right Side of the Deity, symbolizing righteousness and the virtues associated with the deity.
- Diya wick shall face north, which is believed to attract positive energy and spiritual growth, aligning with the direction of Kuber and the Earth's magnetic field.
- Diya shall be circled during Arti of the deity, four times around the feet, two times around the naval, one time around the face, and seven times around the deity's body.

After the Puja, Devotees move their hands over the lamp's flame and touch their eyes and head, symbolizing the reception of divine blessings. The light from the lamp is considered a manifestation of the divine presence, and worshippers seek to absorb the positive energy and blessings radiating from it.

Incense/Dhoop

In Hindu ceremonies, burning incense and dhoop is essential. It's a special way of cleaning the air and making the Puja place sacred. The nice scent is a gift to the Gods, showing our respect and thanks. When we burn incense, it helps us concentrate and think calmly during prayers or meditation. The rising smoke connects us and the divine, carrying our prayers to them.

Each fragrance can be linked to specific gods, creating a special ceremony atmosphere. Gugal and Loban are meaningful scents used in Hindu ceremonies because they are believed to have purifying qualities. When we burn these fragrances, we clean the air and make the place feel holy. Burning the Incense during Pujas is a tradition passed down through generations, connecting our ceremonies to our culture and history.

Puja Mala

A Puja Mala is a string of prayer beads commonly used in Hindu religious practices, particularly during prayer, meditation, and the repetition of sacred mantras. The mala consists of 108 beads, each serving as a counter for reciting the mantra, helping the worshipper maintain focus and concentration. The 109th bead, known as the guru bead, marks the beginning and end of the mala.

During meditation or prayer, practitioners move through the beads in the mala, reciting mantras with each bead. Starting and ending with the Guru bead, they always express gratitude to honor the spiritual teachings and wisdom given by the gurus and teachers.

Using 108 beads in a prayer mala holds scientific and symbolic meaning. It is like a sacred code in Hindu spirituality. It represents everything in the world, both the physical and spiritual parts. This special number is linked to sacred sites, called pithas, and ancient teachings known as Upanishads, showcasing its deep connection to cosmic wisdom.

In the world of stars and planets, Vedic astrology connects 108 to the moon's calendar and the dance between the Earth and the Sun. In yoga, this number relates to 108 energetic pathways called Nadis from the heart center in the body. Mathematically, this mysterious number 108 is like a key opening the door of geometry and calculation about the secrets of some patterns. Its even multiplications make it a harmonious and multifaceted partner in mathematical constructions.

In Hinduism, 108 is a number code that unlocks the universe's secrets, making the Mala a powerful tool for focused prayers, intentions, and connecting with the divine in Hindu traditions.

Rules for the Mala

- The mala should be kept at the heart region.
- The mala should be kept private and stored in a mala bag.
- The mala should never be recited with the index finger.
- The mala should not be changed unless it is broken.
- The mala should never be placed directly on the floor.
- The mala's guru bead should never be crossed while reciting.

Puja Water

In Hindu prayers and ceremonies, offering water carries the profound symbolic significance of hospitality, purification, and a deep devotion to the divine. The water in copper lotas (containers) presented to deities is revered as sacred, accentuating its spiritual importance. Rituals like "Charanamrita" involve using water sanctified by washing the deity's feet, shared with devotees as a divine blessing. Another significant ceremony in Prayers and Havan is Achamana, which transforms water through positive intentions and mantras, symbolizing physical, mental, and spiritual purification. This consecrated water is believed to carry positive energy, playing a vital role in creating a spiritually charged atmosphere and purifying individuals for a meaningful connection with the divine.

These practices collectively emphasize the significance of approaching worship with a pure heart and mind, fostering a meaningful connection with the sacred. Through these symbolic acts, Hindus honor tradition and create an atmosphere that transcends the physical, inviting a deeper spiritual connection.

The Puja Essentials Checklist

This easy checklist is here to guide you through the preparations. Let's make your Puja simple and beautiful while joyfully embracing the traditions.

Puja Thali: To hold offerings and items for every Puja.

Diya/Lamp/Candle: To light during the Puja.

Incense Sticks/Dhoop: To create a fragrant atmosphere during the Puja.

Moli/Sacred Thread: To tie around the wrist as a blessing and protection.

Tilak/Tika: For the forehead, it can be in the form of red powder, Chandan powder, sandalwood powder, or Bhasam.

Unbroken grains of Rice: For applying on tilak/tika.

Ghanti/Bell: For the sacred sound.

Water in copper lotas: For offerings to the deity.

Puja Mala: For Meditation.

Flowers: For offerings to the deity.

Sweets, or Home-Made Prasad/Bhog: For offerings to the deity.

Camphor & Hawan Samagri: For Havan and other prayers.

Red Cloth: For Rituals.

Puja Offerings

In Hindu traditions, offering to the gods is a sacred practice filled with gratitude and devotion. It involves presenting flowers, sweets/bhog/fruits in the form of prayers to acknowledge the divine's role as the source of blessings and guidance in our lives.

Flowers

Offering flowers to deities in Hinduism is a beautiful and meaningful tradition. Flowers symbolize purity and beauty, embodying the essence of our emotions. When we offer flowers during Puja, we offer prana, the life of nature, to the gods. Each type of flower carries a special significance; for example, lotus flowers symbolize purity, Tulsi leaves symbolize devotion, and bel leaves signify dedication. It is generally preferred to offer flowers that have been plucked rather than those found on the ground. Plucking flowers for the deity signifies a conscious and purposeful act of devotion, symbolizing the devotee's effort to select the best and most beautiful offerings for the deity.

Offering flowers is a sacred connection, reminding us of the divine presence in our lives and fostering a sense of humility and appreciation for the beauty around us.

Bhog/Prasad

Bhog in Hindu ceremonies is a heartfelt invitation to share a special meal with the divine, encompassing a delightful array of vegetarian dishes, fruits, sweets, and more. This ritual signifies a harmonious relationship where worshippers acknowledge the divine as the ultimate sustainer of life. Presenting this diverse offering during Bhog is an act of returning the best to the divine, marked by genuine and selfless devotion. The choice of food items can vary based on personal preferences, regional traditions, and the specific deity being honored. Kadah and kheer are common bhog offerings presented during Hindu ceremonies.

Recipes for Prasad

Kadah Prasad:

Here is a simple recipe for four servings.

Ingredients:

- 1 cup wheat flour (atta)
- 1 cup sugar
- 1 cup ghee (clarified butter)
- 3 cups water

Steps:

1. Heat a pan on medium heat and add 1 cup of ghee.
2. Once the ghee melts, add 1 cup wheat flour (atta) to it.
3. Stir continuously and roast the flour in ghee until it turns golden brown and emits a sweet aroma. This might take around 10-12 minutes on low-medium heat.
4. In a separate pot, boil 3 cups of water.
5. Gradually add the boiled water to the roasted flour while stirring continuously to avoid lumps.
6. Cook the mixture on low heat, stirring constantly, until it thickens and reaches a halwa-like consistency.
7. Once the mixture thickens, add 1 cup of sugar and mix well until the sugar dissolves completely.
8. Cook for another 5-7 minutes until the mixture leaves the sides of the pan and reaches a glossy texture.
9. Turn off the heat, and your Kadah Prasad is ready.
10. Garnish with some chopped nuts if desired.

Kheer Prasad:

Here's a simple slow cooker recipe to make Kheer for four servings.

Ingredients:

*   1 litre whole milk
*   1/3 cup basmati rice
*   1/2 cup sugar (adjust to taste)

- A pinch of saffron strands (optional)
- 1/4 teaspoon cardamom powder
- A handful of chopped nuts (almonds, cashews, pistachios) for garnish
- 1 tablespoon ghee (clarified butter)

Steps:

1. Rinse 1/3 cup of basmati rice thoroughly under running water and drain it well.
2. Grease the slow cooker with a bit of ghee to prevent sticking.
3. Pour 1 liter of whole milk into the slow cooker.
4. Add the rinsed rice to the milk in the slow cooker.
5. Cover the slow cooker with its lid and cook on low heat for about 6 hours, stirring occasionally. Ensure the rice is cooked and the milk has thickened.
6. After 6 hours, add 1/2 cup sugar, a pinch of saffron strands (if using), and 1/4 teaspoon cardamom powder. Mix well until the sugar dissolves completely.
7. Continue cooking the kheer in the slow cooker on low heat, uncovered, for 1-2 hours or until it reaches the desired consistency, stirring occasionally.
8. Turn off the slow cooker Once the kheer thickens and attains a creamy texture.
9. Let the kheer cool down and garnish with chopped nuts.

Store Bought Sweets as Prasad/Bhog

Whether homemade or purchased with intention, offering Bhog is a profound way of feeling connected to the divine. When preparing Bhog at home might not be feasible, obtaining sweets from the market is a meaningful alternative. Once offered, the food becomes infused with blessings, transforming our shared enjoyment into a joyous celebration with the divine during ceremonies.

Fruits as Prasad/Bhog

Fruits are considered pure and natural, with life in them, offering the best to the divine presence during ceremonies. A variety of fruits are used in Hindu rituals as offerings or Prasad. Common choices include bananas, apples, oranges, coconuts, and mangoes. The specific fruits used can vary based on personal preferences, regional customs, and the deity being honored during the ceremony. The essence is to offer fresh and pure fruits as a symbol of gratitude and respect to the divine.

How to Perform Puja

Puja is a simple yet meaningful tradition that provides a direct - path to connecting with God. Hindu Puja is a sacred ritual that involves prayers, ceremonies, symbolic gestures, and offerings to communicate with the divine. From chanting mantras to using sacred symbols, Puja is a sensory journey that fosters a deep, timeless connection between worshippers and the divine.

Below, discover steps for Puja, designed for new generations seeking an uncomplicated way to engage in heartfelt and meaningful communication with the divine.

Step 1: Prepare for the Puja

Always shower, Clean, and wear traditional Hindu clothing for festivals and Pujas. This clothing encompasses various styles and garments, each with significance and regional variations. For men, this includes traditional dhotis, kurta-pajamas, or sherwanis, often embellished with intricate embroidery or patterns. Women may wear sarees, lehengas, or salwar kameez adorned with vibrant colors, elaborate designs, and embellishments like zari, sequins, or beadwork.

Step 2: Perform Purification (Shuddhi)

- Start by washing your hands and getting your mind ready for worship.
- Show respect by taking off your shoes and covering your head.
- Use a mat, a clean sheet, or a cushion underneath. Do not sit directly on the floor.

Step 3: Ring the bell

Ring the bell to ward off negative energies and invite positive vibrations into the space.

Step 4: (Avahan) Invocation to the Deity

Take a moment to connect, invite the deity's presence, and seek blessings.

Step 5: Perform Puja Rituals

- Bathe the deities with Ganga Jal or clean water, or symbolically by sprinkling some water on them.
- Adorn deities with beautiful clothes or Moli, the sacred thread.
- Apply the deities Tilak/Tika.
- Offer Flowers or garlands.
- Burn incense.
- Lit Candle or Diya.
- Offer the deity sweets, sugar, fruits, prasad, and water.
- Apply Tilak to everyone.
- Apply Moli to everyone.
- Sing/Chant/Prayer to the deity.

Step 6: Perform Arti

The Sanskrit term 'arti' – from 'aa' (complete) and 'rati' (love) represents our total meditative awareness and devotion to God. With deep reverence, Wave the Lit Lamp in Puja Thali Clockwise while singing, listening, or playing devotional songs. The order is to circle the lamp four times around the deity's feet, two times around the naval, once around the face, and seven times around the body, completing the sacred offering.

Passed among devotees, each person circles the lamp, enriching the ceremony with clapping, bells, and conch shells and deepening the collective connection to the divine.

After Arti is done, soak and offer the blessings from the Lit Lamp. Blessings are taken by moving hands over the lamp's flame and touching eyes and head.

Step 7: Conclude with A Prayer & Seek Blessings

- Conclude the Puja by offering a final round of prayer, expressing gratitude, and seeking blessings from the deity.
- Engage in silent meditation.
- Clean your Hands with water and then spray a few drops of water underneath your seat and touch that water to your forehead after the puja. This is a traditional practice that invites the blessings and benefits of Puja.
- Distribute prasad among family members and guests as a blessing.

Step 8: Maintain Cleanliness and Respect

- After the Puja, clean the area and keep the altar tidy. Properly dispose of used flowers and other offerings by placing them in the garden or plant soil facing north. Alternatively, you can immerse them in flowing water, such as a river or lake. Dispose of the used matches/wicks, which shall never be left in the temple area.

- Once a week, such as on Saturday, devotionally deep cleanse your sacred space. Dust the temple, and gently sprinkle ganga jal or bathe images and the statues of deities. Take the opportunity to converse with the deities, expressing your devotion and gratitude. Dress them in clothes or moli thread, apply tikas to honour their divine presence, and adorn them with flowers. Perform Puja rituals and seek blessings. This sacred practice deepens your spiritual connection, infusing the practice with heartfelt reverence and devotion.

Puja & Prayers Methods

In the hustle of today's life, Puja holds even more significance for both parents and the new generation. For parents, it becomes a timeless tradition to pass on, nurturing tranquillity and spiritual connection within the family. It is a valuable tool for the new generation amid their busy lives, creating a sanctuary of peace and meaningful connection.

Keep your Puja practice simple by incorporating a simple daily Puja in the morning and a simple prayer or meditation in the evening.

Explore traditional Puja on special occasions like birthdays, anniversaries, and festivals, embracing the richness of these moments.

A Simple Daily Puja

Start your morning with a refreshing shower, cleansing both body and mind. Proceed to your dedicated temple to connect with a brief prayer or meditation. Ring the bell. Light the diya and offer water and fruits on the altar as bhog. Offer heartfelt prayers, seeking blessings for the day ahead. After this quick puja, sip the water as sacred prasad from the divine, wash your hands with water and then sprinkle a few drops beneath your seat so the blessings of the puja flow directly to you, and scatter the remaining water around your home to sanctify and bless it. Consume the fruits as prasad blessed by the divine, and share them with your family. This morning puja, though quick, is a deeply meaningful ritual, seamlessly integrating tradition into your busy day.

A Simple Prayer

Find a comfortable spot in your quiet place. Close your eyes gently and breathe in deeply. Picture the deity you're praying to in your mind. Say thank you and express your feelings in your own words. You can also offer a small gesture, like a flower or a moment of silence, to show your devotion. Sit quietly, feeling the connection between you and the divine. When you're ready, slowly open your eyes, carrying the peace of your prayer into the world around you.

A Simple Meditation

Sit comfortably, close your eyes, and take slow breaths. Feel the good energy coming in as you breathe in, and let go of any stress as you breathe out.

Picture the energy flowing with each breath. If your mind wanders, bring it back to your breath. Let go of any distractions and be in the moment. Do this for a few minutes.

After a few minutes, gradually become aware of your surroundings. Open your eyes gently and take a moment to acknowledge the present moment. Stretch if you feel the need and slowly return to your usual activities. Reflect on the calmness and focus you've cultivated during the meditation and carry that sense of peace into the rest of your day.

A Simple Chant

Find a quiet spot, sit comfortably, and close your eyes. Take a deep breath, and chant "Om" slowly and steadily as you exhale. Feel the resonance within your body, breath, soul, and the space around you.

After a few "Om" chants, shift your focus to your breath, letting each chant and breath flow seamlessly. Keep repeating this process, allowing the rhythm of "Om" and your breath to harmonize. Sit quietly as you conclude your Om chanting, appreciating the peace within. Chanting "Om" and focusing on your breath is a simple and calming practice, fostering a deep connection to your inner self and the surrounding space.

A Simple Devotion

It's okay to talk to God in simple words, without fancy language. If you like, you can listen to calming music or prayers on your phone while you pray or do activities such as getting ready for the day. The important thing is to do what feels right for you and help you feel close to God, regardless of the method or formality.

A Simple Arti

As you engage in the beautiful ritual of Arti, often referred to as the ceremony of light, you will wave a lighted wick lamp before the sacred images to channel the Deity's love, energy, and blessings. Use flames from ghee-soaked wicks and complement the ritual with offerings of incense, water, and flowers. This practice honors the Deity and enhances your spiritual connection through the symbolic presentation of these sacred elements.

This particular Arti, which we frequently perform in our Pujas, is dedicated to God Vishnu (Narayan), the sustainer of the Universe.

Arti	Meaning
Om Jai Jagdish Hare	O Lord of the entire universe
Swami Jai Jagdish Hare	Mighty Lord of the entire universe
Bhakt jano ke sankat	The sorrows of devotees
Daas jano ke sankat	The sorrows of followers
Kshan mein door kare	In an instant, you eliminate them
Om Jai Jagdish Hare	O Lord of the entire universe
Joh dhyave phal paave	He who is immersed in devotion

Dukh bin se mann ka	Sadness ceases from his mind
Swami dukh bin se mann ka	Lord, sadness ceases from his mind
Sukh sampati ghar aave	Joy and prosperity will enter the home
Sukh sampati ghar aave	Joy and prosperity will enter the home
Kasht mite tann ka	The problems of the body will go away
Om Jai Jagdish Hare	O Lord of the entire universe
Maat pita tum mere	You are my mother and father
Sharan padhon mein kiski	Whom should I take refuge with
Swami sharan padhon mein kiski	Lord, whom should I take refuge with
Tum bin aur na duja	There is no one else but you
Prabhu bin aur na duja	Lord, there is no one else but you
Aas karoon mein kiski	For whom should I wish
Om Jai Jagdish Hare	O Lord of the entire universe
Tum pooran paramatma	You are the greatest soul
Tum antaryami	You are the omnipotent master
Swami tum antaryami	Lord, you are the omnipotent master
Paar brahm Parmeshwar	Perfect, absolute and supreme God
Paar brahm Parmeshwar	Perfect, absolute and supreme God
Tum sabke swami	You are the Lord of everyone
Om Jai Jagdish Hare	O Lord of the entire universe
Tum karuna ke saagar	You are an ocean of mercy
Tum palan karta	You are the protector

Swami tum palan karta	Lord, you are the protector
Main moorakh khalkhami	I am a simpleton with vain desires
Main sevak tum swami	I am a servant, and you are the Lord
Kripa karo bharta	Grant me thy divine grace
Om Jai Jagdish Hare	O Lord of the entire universe
Vishay vikaar mitaao	Remove faults from the mind
Paap haro deva	Please defeat evil, O Lord
Swami paap haro deva	Lord, please defeat evil
Shradha bhakti badhao	Grow my faith and devotion
Shradha bhakti badhao	Grow my faith and devotion
Santan ki seva	So I can serve the saints
Om Jai Jagdish Hare	O Lord of the entire universe
Tann, mann, dhan sab hai tera	Body, soul, wealth, everything is yours
Swami sab kuch hai tera	Lord, everything is yours
Tera tujhko Arpan	I give everything yours back to you
Tera tujhko Arpan	I give everything yours back to you
Kya lage mera	Nothing is mine
Om Jai Jagdish Hare	O Lord of the entire universe
Om Jai Jagdish Hare	O Lord of the entire universe
Swami Jai Jagdish Hare	Mighty Lord of the entire universe
Bhakt jano ke sankat	The sorrows of devotees
Daas jano ke sankat	The sorrows of followers
Kshan mein door kare	In an instant, you eliminate them
Om Jai Jagdish Hare	O Lord of the entire universe

Puja for Festivals

Each festival has unique rituals that emphasize the importance of respect and devotion. Explore the chapter on festivals to follow the specific rituals performed with reverence, maintaining the sanctity and spiritual significance of the traditions. For Puja, follow the steps of "How to Perform Puja," as outlined in this chapter, taking the time to understand the meaning and purpose behind each ritual. This awareness enhances your connection with the divine and enriches your spiritual experience. If time is limited, follow the steps of "A Simple Daily Puja" with a simple prayer as described under "Puja and Prayer Methods."

While you follow the spiritual path, may your Puja rituals feel close to the divine, turning every time into a special celebration. And to the new generations, keep this tradition alive, letting the Puja flame glow brightly in our beautiful modern world.

Chapter 4

Unlocking the Ancient Chants/Mantras

Mantra practice in Hinduism is deeply rooted in spiritual traditions and has ancient origins across millennia. A mantra or Chant is a repeated word, phrase, or sound used in Hindu puja and meditation to focus the mind, evoke particular energy, or connect with a higher consciousness. It is a tool for achieving a specific wish, clearing obstacles, inviting prosperity, and more.

The Power of Mantras

We feel happy and peaceful when we hear friends' laughter or the gentle rustle of leaves. Even in the quietest moments, a soft hum or a familiar melody can carry a beautiful message, comforting and allowing us to connect deeply.

Chanting is a transformative practice. The sacred sounds we utter profoundly influence our ears, our emotions, and our thoughts. Sound's power transcends what we hear; it resonates within, creating a sacred harmony between the external and internal realms. Sound's vibrations can uplift, heal, and unite us in ways that transcend ordinary words.

The Path of Mantras

The path of chanting invites you to a sacred space where your words and deepest desires intertwine. Seek out specific mantras that align with your intentions, understand their meanings, and incorporate them purposefully into your mantra ritual.

Allow your breath to sync with their rhythm, creating a bridge between your intentions and the powerful cosmic energies they hold.

Let's Embark on this journey with Mantra chanting, a practice that weaves our heartfelt desires into the rhythm of our breath to achieve the desired outcome.

Mantra To Remove Obstacles

This is a Mantra to invoke the Deity Ganesh. Start your day or any new venture by invoking Lord Ganesh, the remover of obstacles. Ask Lord Ganesh for a helping hand through life's twists and turns through this Mantra.

Mantra: "Om Gam Ganapataye Namah"

Meaning: I bow to Lord Ganesh, the remover of obstacles.

Mantra for Spiritual Connection with Shiva

This Mantra is dedicated to the God of the Gods, Mahadev/Shiva. It is widely used in Hindu tradition to invoke a deeper spiritual connection and blessings from Shiva, the God of Transformation.

Mantra: "Om Namah Shivaya"

Meaning: I bow to God Shiva.

Mantra for Spiritual Connection with Narayana

Chanting this Mantra invokes the divine energy of God Narayana, who is considered the preserver and sustainer in Hindu tradition. It is a powerful mantra believed to bring you blessings, protection, and a sense of spiritual connection.

Mantra; "Om Namo Narayana"

Meaning: I Bow to God Vishnu/Narayana.

Mantra to Harmonize & Invite Cosmic Energies

Embrace the essence of the Trimurti mantra, honoring the divine trinity of Brahma, Vishnu, and Shiva. By chanting this Mantra, you can seek balance in your life. Brahma's energy helps to initiate new projects, Vishnu sustains them during challenges, and Shiva ensures necessary transformations and growth.

Mantra: "Om Trimurtaye Namah"

Meaning: I bow to the divine Trimurti.

Mantra For Prosperity

Invoke abundance and prosperity with the Lakshmi mantra, a rhythmic chant to invite the blessings of Lakshmi, the Goddess of wealth, into your life. Let the Mantra resonate, attracting wealth and positive energies for a flourishing journey.

Mantra: "Om Shreem Kamalalaye Namah"

Meaning: I bow to the Goddess of wealth and prosperity.

Mantra For Health

This is a Mantra to invoke Lord Dhanvantrari, the Lord of Medicine and Healing. Allow the harmonious vibrations to nurture your body and spirit, fostering a path to robust health.

Mantra: "Om Dhanvantaraye Namah"

Meaning: I bow to the divine healer, Dhanvantari.

Mantra For Healing from Deadly Ailments

This Mahamrityunjana mantra invokes God Shiva and asks for protection and healing from deadly ailments.

Mantra: "Om Tryambakam Yajamahe Sugandhim Pushtivardhanam

Urva Rukamiva Bandhanan Mrityor Mukshiya Maamritat."

Meaning: I worship the Three-eyed One (Lord Shiva), who is fragrant and nourishes all beings. May He liberate me from the bondage of death and grant me immortality.

Mantra for Spiritual Growth

The Gayatri Mantra, a sacred Vedic verse from the Rigveda, is a doorway to spiritual growth. Dedicated to the deity Savitr, this Mantra invokes blessings for your spiritual enlightenment and wisdom.

Mantra: "Om Bhur Bhuvah Svah, Tat Savitur Varenyam

Bhargo Devasya Dhimahi, Dhiyo Yo Nah Prachodayat"

Meaning: God! You are Omnipresent, omnipotent, and almighty. You are all Light, knowledge, and bliss. You are the Destroyer of fear, the Creator of this Universe, and the Greatest of all. I bow and meditate upon Your light. You guide my intellect in the right direction.

Mantra For Peace

Find tranquillity through this peace mantra, a gentle chant that fosters calmness within. These simple but potent words resonate with soothing vibrations and guide you to a serene space where inner peace becomes a cherished companion.

Mantra: "Om Shanti Shanti Shanti"

Meaning: I invite peace on all levels of existence: Peace in the body, peace in the mind, and peace in the spirit.

Mantra for Protection

The Chamunda mantra is a powerful invocation for strength and protection. This Mantra calls upon the fierce and protective aspect of the Divine Mother, Goddess Chamunda, a formidable and protective form of Goddess Durga, offering you courage, strength, and a shield against negativity.

Mantra: "Om Aim Hrim Klim Chamundaye Vichche"

Meaning: I seek Blessings from Mother Durga to give me a shield of strength and energy to untangle myself from the knots of negativity and evil in my Mind and Body.

How to Recite the Mantra

Before you start, let's understand that this ritual isn't just about saying words; it's about a special connection with your inner self and the divine. By repeating certain sounds or phrases, you create a link with something bigger than yourself. This ancient mantra ritual is a powerful way to evoke and connect with the energy of the Mantra.

The Process

Start your mantra practice by finding a quiet spot and setting a clear intention. Before you begin, please take a moment to understand the chosen mantra, its meaning, and why you're using it. Once you're ready with the chosen Mantra, close your eyes and focus on your breath. Inhale to absorb positive energy and exhale to release distractions, fostering a focused and tranquil state.

The Synchronization

Begin incorporating the sacred mantra, Chant, and align each sacred word intentionally with the natural rhythm of your breath. Picture each word riding the gentle waves of your inhalations and exhalations, creating a seamless dance between breath and mantra. Keep synchronizing the Mantra with your breath. With your exhale, visualize the essence of your intention within the mantra ascending towards the divine, carried by the currents of your breath. Let this sacred melody of your breath, chant, and intent resonate within you. This synchronization will create a profound connection of spiritual alignment. This step lays the foundation for a transformative experience, unlocking the doorway to a harmonious existence.

The Immerse

Now, as you repeat the mantra with a heart full of sacred intention, let yourself fully absorb the depth of this practice. Immerse yourself in the sacred vibes, feeling each repetition echoing through the core of your being. This step is crucial, as it is the heart of your practice. Stay in this special connection for an extended period, allowing the resonance created by the blend of breath and mantra to permeate every aspect of your consciousness. Let time become fluid as you linger in this profound state, experiencing the transformative power of sustained sacred connection.

The Sacred Gratitude

When you sense it's time to conclude, take a sacred pause to acknowledge. Let your mantras' echoes fade, leaving a serene space for introspection. Allow the sacred calmness to linger and let the silence speak.

Conclude your sacred ritual by expressing deep gratitude to the deity. Trust in the sacred process and thank the deity for the sacred energy and guidance received. This last step makes your connection with the spiritual world even more potent, nourishing you spiritually. Carry and maintain this sense of sacred connection you have nurtured through this practice.

Chapter 5

Practicing Traditional Meditations

In the rich tapestry of Hindu traditions, meditation is like an ancient, treasured thread. Woven through the fabric of our culture, it's a practice passed down from our ancestors. Whether we find it in the calm lessons of the Vedas or our peaceful daily practices, meditation is a tradition that has stood the test of time for Hindus. Just like a quiet, sacred ritual, meditation in Hinduism invites us to discover peace within and embrace the spiritual heritage that has been carried through generations.

Meditation Steps

The beauty of meditation lies in its adaptability. Explore techniques that resonate with your spirit, taking things at your own pace. With each step, focus on cultivating a serene atmosphere within. Breathe gently, allowing your mind to create peaceful images and whisper words that feel like soft prayers to the divine. Each step is a relaxed spiritual adventure, drawing you closer to a calming, sacred energy nestled within your very being.

Embodied Presence

Begin by settling comfortably, perhaps in a quiet corner of your home. Sit with a straight spine, and gently close your eyes. In this sacred moment, tune into the divine vessel of your body. Feel its presence; feel the organs, the bones, and every particle that makes you whole. Acknowledge the sacredness within each breath and every heartbeat.

Contemplative Mind

Now, gently shift your focus inward. Observe your thoughts without judgment or attempting to control them. Allow them to flow gracefully, dancing through the serene expanse of your mind for a few sacred minutes. Acknowledge the thoughts and embrace the stillness as you become a mindful observer of your inner world.

Breath of the Divine

Take a deep inhalation, feeling the air fill your lungs. As you exhale slowly through your nose, experience the spirit coursing through each breath. In Hinduism, we revere this breath as Prana, the Life Force, the very energy that sustains us. Breath is considered sacred as it keeps us alive. Recognize the sacredness in each divine breath that fills you, connecting you to a holy rhythm that pulses throughout existence. Breathe with the essence of the spirit, allowing yourself to be enveloped by its presence for a few sacred moments.

Choosing Meditation Path

Embrace a meditation technique that resonates with your spirit. Perhaps it involves focusing on your breath, repeating sacred mantras, or visualizing peaceful scenes. As you engage in your chosen practice, feel the sacred energy flowing through you, connecting you to something greater. Whether whispering sacred words or breathing in the divine essence, allow yourself to experience the oneness that transcends the boundaries of the material world. This communion is a sacred dialogue between your soul and the holy, nurtured by the path you've chosen. Linger in this place for as long as feels right, letting time melt away as you find solace and connection within.

Closing Blessing

When you feel ready to conclude, sit quietly, absorbing the divine aftereffects of your meditation. Feel the lingering presence of the sacred within and around you. Allow gratitude to fill your heart, recognizing the sanctity of this time and the connection forged with the divine during these sacred moments.

Exploring the Subtle Body and Kundalini Energy

Let's explore the nature of our being: the physical body and the subtle body. The physical body is the tangible form we experience in the material world. It is made up of cells, tissues, and organs and functions through biological processes. The subtle body, on the other hand, is the non-physical, energetic aspect of our being, composed of koshas (layers), chakras, and nadis through which the divine life force flows.

The subtle energetic body acts like a sacred bridge that transcends physical limitations and interacts with higher consciousness. It is intricately connected to the divine feminine Shakti, the Kundalini energy, which lies dormant at the base of the spine, waiting to awaken and rise through this subtle energetic body to meet and unite with Shiva, the cosmic higher consciousness. Kundalini awakening is seen as the process of spiritual enlightenment and self-realization.

For the process, it is crucial to understand the Nadis (energetic channels), chakras (energy centers), and koshas (spiritual layers) of the subtle body.

Envision Nadis as pathways, chakras as vibrant wheels inside the body, and koshas as layers like spiritual blankets around them. This understanding will prepare you for a profound and transformative meditation experience.

Navigating the Koshas

Koshas are like layers that cover who we are. From our physical body to our inner joy, each layer is essential. Exploring these layers helps us understand ourselves better and feel more connected spiritually.

Body Layer (Annamaya Kosha): As you take a moment to breathe, feel the aliveness in your body. The body is a vessel, a unique form given to you for a grand spiritual adventure.

Energy Layer (Pranamaya Kosha): Close your eyes and sense the air filling your lungs. Imagine it as more than just breath—it's a sacred energy, a connection to a universal energy that keeps you alive and in harmony with the sacred pulse of the universe.

Thought Layer (Manomaya Kosha): Delve into your inner thoughts. See them not just as passing ideas but as the brushstrokes shaping a sacred painting within you. It's a dance of emotions and thoughts, creating your spiritual journey.

Wisdom Layer (Vijnanamaya Kosha): Imagine sitting in a quiet space within yourself. This is your seat of understanding, not just facts but a source of deep wisdom. Feel it gently guiding you on your spiritual path.

Joyful Layer (Anandamaya Kosha): Take a journey within, to the core of your being. There, discover a serene space filled with pure joy. Let this be your experience of the divine inside you and all around you.

In simplicity, these layers form the sacred fabric of your being, each one contributing to your spiritual journey. These five unique yet interconnected koshas weave the sacred tapestry of who you are. Understanding them allows you to nurture each layer, fostering your spiritual journey.

Channeling the Nadis (Energetic Channels)

In Hindu spiritual traditions, the Ida, Pingala, and Sushumna nadis are essential to the flow of prana (life force) and the awakening of kundalini energy.

Prana is the vital life force that sustains and energizes all living beings and the universe. Flowing through pathways called nadis, such as Ida, Pingala, and Sushumna, prana regulates physical and mental functions, including health and vitality. In spiritual practices like yoga and meditation, prana is harnessed and balanced to promote personal growth and achieve higher states of consciousness.

The Ida nadi, associated with the moon and feminine energy, runs along the left side of the spine, embodying calmness and intuition. The Pingala nadi, linked to the sun and masculine energy, traverses the right side, representing vitality and logic. The central Sushumna nadi becomes the pathway for the rising kundalini energy, depicted as a coiled serpent at the base of the spine, which ascends through Sushumna, moving through the chakras and leading to profound spiritual enlightenment.

A meticulous balance of the nadis, combined with dedicated, patient engagement in the full spectrum of Yoga's practices, purifies and aligns the energetic channels. This allows prana to flow freely and supports the journey toward inner harmony and spiritual awakening. Such harmonious energy flow reflects a deep commitment to spiritual growth, facilitating the rise to higher states of consciousness and the ultimate experience of oneness with the divine.

Navigating the Chakras

Now, let's explore the seven primary chakras, energy centers aligned along your spine. Each chakra is associated with a specific location and a set of attributes. Imagine each chakra as a vibrant vortex with its unique color and Bija (seed) chant/mantra, representing the essence of that energy center.

We often find ourselves anchored in the lower chakras, where basic instincts and material desires dominate. However, the true spiritual journey lies in rising above these energies and progressing upward through the higher chakras, each representing elevated states of awareness and connection. This ascent culminates at the Sahasrara Chakra, the crown center, where we unite with higher consciousness and experience ultimate oneness with the divine.

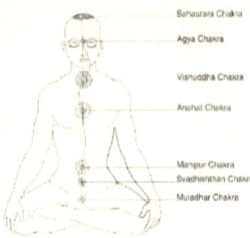

Root Chakra (Muladhar): Muladhar is located at the base of the spine. It grounds you to the Earth, ensuring stability and security.

Sacral Chakra (Swadhisthan): Swadhisthan is positioned in your lower abdomen. It's linked to creativity, sensuality, and emotional well-being.

Solar Plexus Chakra (Manipur): Manipur is located in your upper abdomen. Manipur influences your personal power, confidence, and self-esteem.

Heart Chakra (Anahat): Anahat is found at the center of your chest. Anahat embodies love, compassion, and your capacity for meaningful relationships.

Throat Chakra (Vishuddh): Vishuddh is situated in the throat region. Vishuddh guides communication, self-expression, and your truth.

Third Eye Chakra (Ājñā): Ājñā is positioned between your eyebrows and is linked to intuition, perception, and spiritual awareness.

Crown Chakra (Sahasrar): Sahasrar is located at the top of your head. It connects us to the divine and fosters spiritual enlightenment.

The Kundalini Meditation Technique

Rooted in ancient yogic traditions, this practice unfolds like a sacred dance of energy within, stirring the dormant serpent power or Kundalini coiled at the base of the spine. Kundalini meditation is a sacred communion, inviting practitioners to harmonize breath, movement, and mantra, creating a celestial symphony that awakens the soul. It is not merely a meditation but a sacred pilgrimage within to unlock the hidden treasures of consciousness.

Important Reminder

Kundalini's energy is a profound and potent force that demands deep respect and careful guidance. Awakening this energy is a challenging endeavor, often requiring the wisdom of a skilled guru. Without such guidance, one must approach this practice with utmost caution.

A thorough cleansing of body, mind, and spirit is essential to awaken Kundalini. This journey involves a deep realization of our connection to the cosmos, recognizing the role of energy within us, and understanding our integral place in the universe. The tools for this spiritual awakening reside within, as the universe is mirrored inside us. By embracing this inner consciousness and walking the path of self-realization, we unlock the profound potential that aligns us with the cosmic essence and moves us toward moksha, or liberation.

Prepare

Find a quiet, comfy space where you won't be disturbed. Sit comfortably with a straight back. Become aware of your surroundings.

Connect

Take a moment to pass through the layers of your being, known as koshas.

➤ Begin with the Annamaya Kosha, your physical body, appreciating its unique form and vitality. Take time to notice the body from head to toe. Acknowledge each and every part of the body.

➤ Move inward to the Pranamaya Kosha, acknowledging the sacred energy of your breath. Notice each breath going in and out of the body. Just follow the breath, listen to the breath, and become one with the breath. Take a few balancing Pranayama breaths.

➤ Now, we transition to the Manomaya Kosha, a place of thoughts and emotions. Notice what thoughts are coming into the mind. Just observe and let them go like clouds. Become the observer to watch those thoughts come and go. Stay here for a minute and just observe.

- Now, go deeper and find the Vijnanamaya Kosha, where deep wisdom resides. Connect with this layer to acknowledge your journey of discovering your spiritual truth. Take a moment to acknowledge the sacred journey you are on.
- Beneath, find the Anandamaya Kosha, the innermost layer, representing bliss and the connection to the divine. Enjoy this place where you are truly connected to your essence. Stay here for a few sacred breaths. Seek permission from your true self, your soul, to go through this journey.

You are establishing this connection with your true self so that you can meditate more deeply.

Awaken

Picture roots extending from your spine, grounding you like sturdy anchors. Feel the comforting stability and connection to the Earth beneath you. Notice that You are firmly grounded. Now, visualize a coiled serpent at the base of your spine. Take a pause and seek permission from the kundalini energy to enter the awakening process.

Feel the awakening of the Kundalini energy. See the serpent energy stirring and getting ready to ascend. Call upon this energy as you chant. Put an intention behind it and say it loudly or inside.

As I chant, I humbly invoke the awakening of the Root Muladhar Chakra. With each breath, I feel its energy rising; I call forth the awakening with the chant (Lam).

Chant "Lam" a few times and concentrate on the base of the spine. See the red energy at the base of your spine connecting with Earth's grounding forces.

As you repeat the chant Lam, feel the first chakra at the base of your spine opening clockwise, and feel the gentle rise of energy from that center going upwards.

The energy ascends towards the lower belly, below the navel. Staying connected to the energy, say: "I humbly ask you to awaken the Sacral Swadhisthan Chakra." With each breath, I feel its energy rising; I call forth the awakening with the chant (Vam).

Chant: "Vam" a few times and concentrate on the lower abdomen.

Focus and connect to the orange energy as it opens your sacral chakra clockwise.

Sense the rise and spread of energy, unleashing passion. Stay here for a few moments, and keep chanting Vam, feeling the passion of the energy.

Ascending upwards towards the upper abdomen, feel the energy changing color to yellow-golden. Say, "I chant to illuminate the Manipur Solar Chakra." With each breath, I feel its energy rising; I call forth the awakening with the chant (Ram).

Chant: "Ram" a few times and focus on the upper abdomen.

Shift your attention as you notice the energy opening up your solar chakra and turning to a bright golden color in your upper abdomen.

Feel the radiating warmth of the energy empowering your inner strength. Connect and stay here with the warmth of the energy. Keep chanting, Ram.

Experience the expansion of energy towards the chest. Gaze directly inside your chest and see the energy transforming into a green color. See it radiating from your Anahat, Heart Chakra.

Invoke and say, "May my chants open the Anahat Chakra." With each breath, I feel its energy expanding; I call forth the awakening with the chant (Yam).

Chant: "Yam" a few times and focus on the heart chakra opening clockwise.

Feel the energy filling the space beyond the heart center, ready to ascend towards the throat center. Say it loud: "With my chants, I invoke the Vishuudh, Throat Chakra." With each breath, I feel its energy rising; I call forth the awakening with the chant (Ham).

Chant: "Ham" a few times and concentrate on your throat. Feel the serpentine energy changing from green to blue color at your throat. Let this energy open your throat chakra and chant several times, "Ham."

Stay connected to the blue energy, and slowly ascend towards the third eye center between your eyebrows. Focus on your Ājñā, Third Eye Center.

Feel the energy changing color to indigo, the dark blue-purple pulsing at the third eye center. Feel the spread and ascension of pulsing energy all around you.

Chant Om several times and feel the sacred connection to the third eye center. Say loud, "I call upon the Ājñā, Third Eye Chakra to awaken." With each breath, I feel its energy stirring; I call forth the awakening with the chant (Om).

Keep chanting "Om" and connect to open the third eye chakra, circling clockwise between eyebrows.

Direct your attention to your crown as you experience the kundalini energy rising to the crown and changing to white. You also experience the vibrations of this energy at the top of your head. Chant "Om" and feel the forging of a sacred link with higher realms.

Say it silently, "I call upon the Sahasrar, Crown Chakra, to open and connect me to the divine." With each breath, I feel its energy rising and opening my crown; I call forth the awakening with the chant (Om).

Keep chanting Om several times here, allowing it to open your crown chakra clockwise, concentrating on the white light at the top of your head.

Now, feel this serpent energy from the base of the spine piercing through each chakra and radiating upwards to the universe in white light. Feel all your chakras circling clockwise, pulsing with this serpent energy inside.

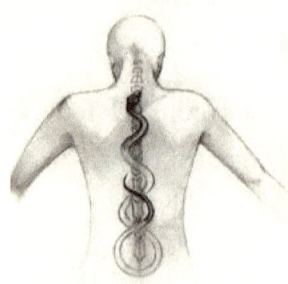

Breath in Sync

Synchronize your breath with the serpent energy's movements. Inhale as the energy rises, exhale as it descends, piercing and opening the chakras. Feel the natural rhythm guiding this Kundalini energy. Let the breath linger in the awakened energy, and maintain the sync for a few moments.

Inhale as it rises and exhale as it descends. Keep breathing in the energy. With Inhale, it ascends, and with exhale, it descends.

Harmonious Descent

Stay immersed in this energy, allowing the resonance of each activated chakra to permeate you for a few sacred minutes.

It's time for the energy to descend gracefully. Take a moment to express gratitude to the kundalini energy, appreciating its role in the opening, balancing, and healing of the chakras and the body. With the descent, this divine energy revisits each chakra.

At the Crown Sahasrar, Chakra, express gratitude for the opening and allow the energy to close the chakra delicately, envisioning its sealing radiating white.

Direct the descent of the energy to the Ājñā, the Third Eye Chakra, express gratitude for the opening and healing, and permit the energy to close and seal this balanced dark blue/violet-colored center gracefully.

As the energy continues the journey to the Vishuddh, the Throat Chakra, express heartfelt thanks for the opening and healing as you allow the balanced Blue Thorat chakra to close and seal gently.

Descend further to the Anahat, the Heart Chakra, expressing profound gratitude for the opening and healing it has received, letting the energy tenderly close the balanced green heart chakra.

Continue this celestial descent to the upper abdomen of Manipur, the Solar Plexus Chakra, offering gratitude for the opening and allowing the energy to close this balanced, yellow chakra gracefully.

As the energy arrives at the Swadhisthan, the Sacral Chakra in the lower abdomen expresses gratitude for its opening and healing and witnesses the energy tenderly closing the orange chakra, like the closing of a sacred book.

Finally, express gratitude as the energy reaches the Muladhar, the Root Chakra, letting it gently close, like the comforting embrace of the earth. Let the energy tenderly close the Red Root Chakra, completing this sacred cycle with gratitude and serenity.

Let the serpent energy rest at the base, coiled and ready for future awakening. Notice the earth below you, grounding you. Feel yourself supported by the grounding earth energies. Stay here for a few breaths.

Notice your body and the natural rhythm of the breath. When you are ready, bring your awareness back to the present. Open your eyes and sense the harmonized energy radiating from your body. Bask in this integrated state, feeling the radiant energy of each chakra for a few minutes before gently transitioning to the daily activities.

In the gentle embrace of Kundalini meditation, remember that this sacred energy lies dormant within, patiently awaiting your conscious connection. Whether guided or observed, the activation of Kundalini is a process approached with respect, not fear. It is a divine force residing in us, a dormant power ready to be awakened.

Recognize that this transformative path demands an unwavering commitment to all eight limbs of yogic practices. Embrace the journey with unwavering dedication and patience as it leads to profound spiritual enlightenment, symbolizing the union of dynamic energy (Shakti) with consciousness (Shiva) at the crown chakra.

Mudra Meditation

As you embrace meditation, deepen your connection. Spend more time in peaceful contemplation, allowing serenity to unfold naturally. Explore mudras and sacred hand gestures to enhance your practice and align your mind, body, and spirit holistically.

- Take a comfortable seat, straighten your spine, and gently close your eyes. In this sacred moment, tune into your body's divine vessel. Feel its presence, the organs, the bones, and all the particles that make up the body. Acknowledge the sacredness within every breath and every heartbeat.

- Turn your focus inward, observing your thoughts without judgment or interference. Allow them to come gracefully dance in the serene space of your mind for a few sacred minutes. Acknowledge the thoughts and embrace the stillness as you become a mindful observer of your inner world.

- Inhale deeply, exhale slowly through the nose and sense the spirit within each breath. In Hinduism, we call Breath, Prana, Life Force, and Energy. Breath is considered sacred as it keeps us alive. Acknowledge this life force in each divine breath that fills you, connecting you to a sacred rhythm. Breathe with the essence of the spirit, immersing yourself in its presence for a few sacred moments.

- Choose the Mudra. Understand the meaning and understand the purpose of mudra. Once your hands and fingertips make mudra and touch, sense the sacred energy between your hands. Close your eyes and set a pure intention, perhaps seeking inner tranquillity or a connection with the sacred. Picture the sacred energy forming a gentle loop between your hands. Silently repeat words that feel sacred and aligned with your intention. Feel the serene flow of this sacred energy and be aware of any peaceful sensations. Continue in this sacred state for 5-10 minutes.

- When you sense the time is right to conclude, sit in quiet reflection and gently open your eyes. Take a moment to feel the lingering energy between your hands. Let gratitude fill your heart, acknowledging the sacredness of this time and the profound connection woven with the divine through the mudras.

You've woven a sacred tapestry of connection in the simplicity of touch and intention. I have included a selection of a few mudras, each with its unique essence. They are ready to guide you on a profound journey within. Choose the one that resonates with your spirit, and let the subtle language of mudras guide your meditative voyage.

Anjali Mudra (Prayer)

To perform the Anjali Mudra, bring your hands together at the heart center, palms touching, and fingers pointing upward. Gently press the palms against each other. This mudra symbolizes respect and acknowledgment of the divine within and around you.

Benefits: This gesture opens your heart, fostering emotional well-being and a harmonious connection with those around you.

Gyan Mudra (Wisdom)

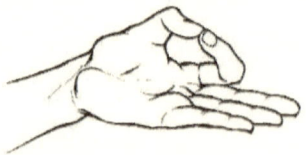

To practice the Gyan Mudra, sit comfortably and touch the tip of your index finger to the tip of your thumb, creating a gentle circle and a connection. Allow the other three fingers to extend gracefully.

Benefits: This mudra enhances concentration, stimulates knowledge, and invites a sense of spiritual insight.

Shuni Mudra (Patience)

For the Shuni Mudra, bring the tip of your middle finger to the tip of your thumb while keeping the other three fingers straight.

Benefits: This mudra is associated with patience and helps quiet the mind. Regular practice of this mudra helps in developing resilience, improving concentration, and cultivating a balanced and grounded mindset. It is particularly beneficial for those seeking inner strength and mental stability.

As we embrace the simplicity and profound benefits of these sacred hand gestures, let them be a timeless tool for today's seekers. May the essence of mudra meditation resonate with the hearts and minds of the new generation, offering a pathway to inner calm and balance in the midst of the modern whirlwind.

Mala Beads Meditation

Discover Mala Beads Meditation, a simple yet powerful practice. Each bead offers a touch that helps anchor your focus. As you trace the beads through your fingers, feel the sacred energy they carry, grounding you in the present moment. Let the quiet rustle of beads guide you into a serene space of inner reflection and tranquillity.

Traditionally, Malas are crafted from Rudraksha beads, which are highly revered in Hinduism. Rudraksha beads are believed to possess sacred and divine qualities, making them a symbol of spiritual power. Malas may also include tulsi, sandalwood, gemstones, or crystals, each carrying specific energies and meanings. Choose a mala that resonates with your heart.

The mala consists of 108 beads, each serving as a counter for reciting the mantra, helping the worshipper maintain focus and concentration. The 109th bead, known as the guru bead, marks the beginning and end of the mala.

Using 108 beads in a prayer mala holds scientific and symbolic meaning. It is like a sacred code in Hindu spirituality. It represents everything in the world, both the physical and spiritual parts. This special number is linked to sacred sites, called pithas, and ancient teachings known as Upanishads, showcasing its deep connection to cosmic wisdom.

In the world of stars and planets, Vedic astrology connects 108 to the moon's calendar and the dance between the Earth and the Sun. In yoga, this number relates to 108 energetic pathways called nadis from the heart center in the body. Mathematically, this mysterious number 108 is like a key opening the door of geometry and calculation about the secrets of some patterns. Its even multiplications make it a harmonious and multifaceted partner in mathematical constructions.

In Hinduism, 108 is a number code that unlocks the universe's secrets, making the Mala a powerful tool for focused prayers, intentions, and connecting with the divine in Hindu traditions.

Rules for the Mala

- The mala should be kept at the heart region.

- The mala should be kept private and stored in a mala bag.

- The mala should never be recited with the index finger.

- The mala should not be changed unless it is broken.

- The mala should never be placed directly on the floor.

- The mala's guru bead should never be crossed while reciting.

Meditation Technique

Once you have chosen your mala, choose a mantra (Refer to the Chapter Unlocking the Chants/Mantras) or choose a simple mantra such as Om or Om Namah Shivaya. Repeat the mantra with each bead, infusing your meditation with sincere devotion.

- Hold your mala with one hand.
- Let it drape across your fingers so you can move it easily. Please make sure that the mala stays above your Naval region.
- Start at the Guru bead and acknowledge your teachers and gurus before starting the process.
- Move your fingers to the next bead, breathing in and out once per bead.
- Chant your chosen mantra with each bead.
- Finish at the guru bead to complete 108 breaths.

In wrapping up our journey with Mala Beads, imagine these sacred strands as gentle guides for the new generation. Let each bead remind us to pause, breathe, and find tranquillity amidst the busyness of life. May the simple act of touching these beads become a source of calm and connection for the seekers of today and tomorrow.

Bhramari Meditation

Bhramari meditation is a special meditation inspired by the buzzing sound of a bee, known as Bhramari. The word "Bhramari" means "bee" in Sanskrit. In this meditation, you make a humming sound while breathing out, similar to the gentle hum of bees. This meditation reduces stress, calms the mind, and promotes inner peace.

The humming in Bhramari meditation represents the calm hum of creation, linking those who practice it to the natural rhythms of the universe. The practice acknowledges the vital energy in the sound vibrations, which resonate within the body and mind, fostering a profound sense of harmony.

Bhramari Meditation Technique

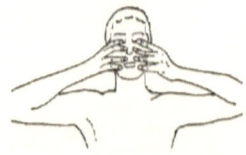

Below, you can find the practice of Bhramari meditation, a powerful technique designed to calm the mind and rejuvenate the spirit.

Create Quite

Choose a quiet and comfortable place to sit. You can sit cross-legged on the floor or in a chair with your spine straight. Take a moment to relax, take a few breaths, and when ready, close your eyes. Take a few more focused deep breaths to relax your body and mind. Release tension from your shoulders, neck, and face.

Hand Positions

Place your hands on your face, with one thumb on each tongue like projection of the outer ear. The index fingers should lightly touch the inner corners of your eyes, the middle fingers on the sides of the nose, the ring fingers above the lips, and the pinkies just below.

The Sound

Inhale deeply through your nose, filling your lungs with air. As you exhale, produce a steady, humming sound. Allow the sound to be smooth and continuous, similar to the buzzing of a bee. Continue humming throughout the entire exhalation.

After completing one humming exhalation, take a moment to inhale deeply again through your nose and repeat the humming sound. Feel the vibration in your head and chest. This intentional breath cycle contributes to the overall calming effect of Bhramari meditation, bringing a harmonious balance between the soothing hum and the rejuvenating inhalation.

As you finish Bhramari meditation, feel the calm hum stay with you. Slowly open your eyes, thankful for this peaceful pause. Let the soothing vibes linger, bringing a sense of calm to your day.

Tratak (Candle Gazing) Meditation

Step into Tratak Meditation, a practice rooted in focus and stillness. Tratak, meaning "gazing" in Sanskrit, invites you to gaze at a single point, like a candle flame. This simple yet powerful technique cultivates concentration and mental focus, guiding you into inner peace and contemplation.

Meditation Technique

Tratak meditation is a focused and powerful technique that can enhance concentration, calm the mind, and deepen one's meditation experience.

Prepare Your Space

Find a dark, quiet and comfortable space with minimal distractions. Sit in a comfortable position with your spine straight. Select a specific point to gaze at. This could be a candle flame, diya or a symbol. Ensure the point is at eye level.

Hold the Gaze

- If using a candle, place it at a comfortable distance in front of you, such as four to five feet.
- Ensure the flame is steady, not affected by drafts, and is at eye level.

- Focus your gaze on the candle flame without blinking.
- Keep your eyes open and try to maintain a soft focus.
- Initially, your eyes may water or feel strained. Resist the urge to blink excessively.
- Continue gazing at the chosen point for as long as possible.
- If your eyes water excessively or become strained, close them briefly and resume.

Maintain Inner Stillness

As you gaze, aim to still your mind. Allow thoughts to come and go without attaching to them. If your mind wanders, gently bring your focus back to the point.

Closing the Practice

After an extended period of gazing, close your eyes gently. With closed eyes, try to visualize the afterimage of the candle or the symbol in your mind's eye. Spend a few moments in silent reflection, internalizing the effects of the serene connection between your gaze and inner calm. Adjust the duration based on your comfort, gradually increasing it as you become more accustomed to the practice.

Likhit Jaap/ Mantra Writing Meditation

Writing a mantra 108 times is a powerful spiritual practice rooted in ancient traditions. The number 108 is sacred in many spiritual disciplines, symbolizing the wholeness of existence. This repetitive act serves as meditation, focusing the mind, deepening concentration, and cultivating inner peace. It reinforces the mantra's vibrations, purifies the mind, and enhances devotion and mindfulness.

Countless sacred mantras serve as gateways to deeper meditation and spiritual writing, such as "राम" (Raam), "ॐ" (Aum), "ॐ नमः शिवाय" (Aum Namah Shivaya), "हरी ॐ" (Hari Om), and many others. Begin your journey by selecting a mantra that speaks to the core of your being. As your spiritual path unfolds, allow your practice to expand by embracing additional mantras, each adding its unique vibration to your evolving inner harmony.

Mantra Writing Technique

We will immerse ourselves in the Om mantra, delving into its profound spiritual energy and significance. Whether you choose to write the mantra in English or Sanskrit, let your expression be intentional and filled with devotion, honoring its deep spiritual resonance.

IN SANSKRIT

ॐ ॐ ॐ ॐ ॐ ॐ ॐ ॐ ॐ ॐ

ॐ ॐ ॐ ॐ ॐ ॐ ॐ ॐ ॐ ॐ

ॐ ॐ ॐ ॐ ॐ ॐ ॐ ॐ ॐ ॐ

ॐ ॐ ॐ ॐ ॐ ॐ ॐ ॐ ॐ ॐ

IN ENGLISH

Aum Aum Aum Aum Aum Aum Aum Aum Aum Aum

Aum Aum Aum Aum Aum Aum Aum Aum Aum Aum

Aum Aum Aum Aum Aum Aum Aum Aum Aum Aum

Aum Aum Aum Aum Aum Aum Aum Aum Aum Aum

Begin by finding a quiet and comfortable place where you can sit undisturbed. Gather your materials: a notebook and a pen, which are reserved specifically for this practice.

Take a few deep breaths to center yourself, allowing any distractions to fade away. As you begin, write the word "Om" with mindful intention, letting each stroke of the pen be an act of devotion. Feel the sacred vibration of "Om" resonate within you as you write, allowing its spiritual significance to permeate your consciousness. Continue this process with steady focus, writing "Om" 108 times, each repetition deepening your connection to the divine sound.

This practice not only calms the mind but also aligns your energy with the universal vibration, bringing a sense of peace and inner harmony.

As you complete the 108th "Om," take a moment to sit in silence, absorbing the stillness and tranquillity that follow. Feel the serene energy flow through you, carrying the sacred essence of "Om" into your day.

Note: Once filled, this book or journal becomes a cherished record of your spiritual journey. It stands as a testament to your devotion and growth, providing ongoing inspiration and guidance. Whether kept in a sacred space or revisited frequently, may it serve as a lasting source of wisdom and spiritual enrichment.

In the serene practice of meditation, let us honor the importance of seeking guidance from a teacher whose wisdom enriches our journey. May we continue to tread this path with reverence, finding peace and connection within and beyond.

Chapter 6

Exploring the Classical Path of Yoga

Embracing the traditional and ancient practice of yoga has become vital in today's fast-paced world. It offers a holistic approach, addressing not just our physical well-being but also our mental and spiritual needs. The word "yoga" itself translates to "union," signifying the practice's core principle bringing together the body and mind for a sense of wholeness.

In its traditional form, yoga is a holistic system, but in Western cultures, it can sometimes be more focused on physical postures (asanas) and less on the broader spiritual aspects. So, while Western interpretations exist, exploring yoga in its traditional context offers a richer and more holistic understanding of this ancient practice.

Yoga is a progressive journey with eight essential steps that equip us with tools to cultivate kindness, maintain physical health, manage stress, and achieve a deep sense of inner peace.

Eight Steps (Limbs) of Yoga

Yoga is more than just physical postures; it is a guide for our mind, body, and spirit. Let's gently navigate through the eight limbs of yoga, discovering how these ancient principles can be embraced daily in a way that resonates with the simplicity and authenticity of our daily lives.

1. Yama (Ethical Guidelines)

The foundation of yoga practice rests on Yama, the five ethical guidelines that encourage us to become better individuals and contribute positively to society. These principles include:

a. **Ahimsa (non-harming):** Treat all living beings with kindness and respect, avoiding violence in thought, word, and action.

b. **Satya (Truthfulness)**: Be honest and truthful in your interactions, fostering trust and authenticity in your actions.

c. **Asteya (non-stealing):** Abstain from taking what doesn't belong to you. It cultivates a sense of fairness and respect for others' possessions.

d. **Brahmacharya (Moderation):** Practice self-control and moderation in your desires and impulses, leading to a balanced and fulfilling life.

e. **Aparigraha (Non-possessiveness)**: Cultivate contentment with what you have; find joy in simplicity and avoid excessive attachment to material possessions.

These principles form the foundation of the first limb in practicing yoga, guiding us to be reasonable and fair individuals and ultimately contributing to making the world a better place.

2. Niyama (Personal Disciplines)

Building upon the foundation of Yama, Niyama is our friendly discipline coach for a more balanced and joyful life. Let's delve into these five simple yet powerful principles that can bring the essence of disciplined living into your daily moments.

a. **Saucha (Cleanliness)**: Maintain physical cleanliness through regular bathing and a tidy environment. Additionally, strive for inner cleanliness by letting go of negative thoughts and emotions.

b. **Santosha (Contentment):** Practice being happy and appreciative of what you already have. Finding joy and contentment in what you already have fosters peace and well-being.

c. **Tapas (Discipline and Effort):** Develop dedication and perseverance in your endeavors. Your unwavering discipline is the key to your personal and spiritual growth.

d. **Svadhyaya (Self-Study)**: Spend a few moments reflecting on your strengths and motivations. In addition, explore interesting literature to expand your knowledge and perspective.

e. **Ishvara Pranidhana (Surrender):** Cultivate a sense of faith and trust in a higher power or the flow of life. Accepting what is outside your control fosters peace and reduces anxiety.

By following Niyama, we infuse discipline into our life's journey, turning simplicity into a powerful guide for self-discovery and fulfillment.

3. Asana (Physical Postures)

The third limb of yoga is Asana, which involves practicing various physical postures. It means moving and holding different body positions that help strengthen and balance the body and mind.

People practice Asana not just for exercise but because it helps create a comfortable and steady posture, which is vital for meditation and finding inner peace. So, when we talk about different Asanas, we bring awareness to our bodies, learning to control and align them with intention. This practice can also be deeply therapeutic, releasing tension and promoting relaxation.

4. Pranayama (Breath Control)

Pranayama, the fourth limb of yoga, is like the art of breathing with purpose. Pranayama involves using different techniques to lengthen, deepen, and control your breath. It's like unlocking the power of your breath for various benefits calming the mind, boosting energy, promoting focus, and, most importantly, achieving spiritual benefits. Techniques like Nadi Shodhana, Kapalabhati, Anulom Vilom, Bhramari, Sheetali, and Ujjayi are profound in their own right. While there are numerous pranayama techniques mentioned earlier, our focus will be on two foundational practices: Kapalabhati and Anulom Vilom.

a. **Kapalabhati**

Begin by sitting comfortably with a straight spine and relaxed shoulders. Take a deep breath in, filling your lungs completely. As you exhale forcefully and sharply through your nose, contract your abdominal muscles in a quick and rhythmic manner. The inhalation should happen passively as your abdomen relaxes. Start with a few rounds and gradually increase the pace and duration as you build stamina. Kapalabhati cleanses the respiratory system, energizes the body, and clears the mind.

b. **Anulom Vilom**

Sit in a comfortable position with your spine erect and close your eyes. Close your right nostril with your right thumb and inhale deeply through the left nostril. Then, close the left nostril with your ring finger and release the right nostril, exhaling slowly and completely. Inhale through the right nostril, then switch to close the right nostril with the thumb and release the ring finger to exhale through the left. This completes one cycle. Continue alternating nostrils, focusing on smooth, deep breaths. Anulom Vilom balances the nervous system, enhances respiratory efficiency, and promotes mental clarity.

Practice these pranayama techniques with mindfulness and patience, gradually increasing duration and intensity as you become more comfortable. Regular practice of Kapalabhati and Anulom Vilom can significantly improve your overall health and well-being, bringing harmony to both body and mind.

5. Pratyahara (Withdrawal of Senses)

 In traditional teachings, Pratyahara involves withdrawing the senses from external stimuli. It's about learning to manage our senses rather than being controlled by them. Think of Pratyahara as your guide to mastering your senses in today's busy world. Here are some simple ways to incorporate Pratyahara into your daily routine:

a. **Sight**: Find a quiet spot away from screens and close your eyes. With Pratyahara, you consciously give your mind a break from visual stimuli.
b. **Hearing:** Step away from noisy environments. Whether you cover your ears with your hands or listen to your breath, Pratyahara helps you choose what sounds to focus on, bringing a sense of calm.

c. **Smell:** Pay attention to the scents around you. Focus on calming smells like fresh air, rain, flowers, or essential oils. Pratyahara lets you decide which smells affect your mood, creating a more intentional experience.

d. **Taste:** When you eat, enjoy each bite. Control your eating speed, focusing on the flavors without rushing. Pratyahara guides you in controlling your connection with food, making your meals more mindful.

e. **Touch:** Feel your ground beneath your feet or your breath against your nostrils. Pratyahara encourages you to be intentional about the sensations affecting your mind.

By trying these simple practices, you're doing Pratyahara—taking charge and withdrawing your senses from the busy world. It's like being the captain of your ship, navigating through life with a calm and focused mind.

6. Dharana (Concentration)

Focus on one thing at a time. Think of Dharana, the sixth limb of yoga, as concentrating all your attention on a chosen object, thought, or sensation. This could be the rise and fall of your chest as you breathe, a mantra silently repeated in your mind, or a captivating flame flickering before you. The mind naturally wanders, flitting from one thought to another. Dharana teaches you to gently guide your attention back to your chosen point of focus, training the mind for increased concentration and mental clarity. Incorporating Dharana into daily life is easier than you might think. It involves giving your complete focus to one task, whether it's work, reading, or enjoying a meal. This simple yet profound practice helps bring a sense of calm and clarity to your daily activities, following the traditional path of yoga to center the mind and nurture inner peace.

7. Dhyana (Meditation)

Dhyana, often referred to as meditation, builds upon the foundation laid by Dharana. Having learned to focus our attention, we now strive for continuous, effortless concentration.

It's like letting your mind gently flow without interruption. In daily life, Dhyana means carving out moments to sit quietly, focus on your breath, and let go of distractions. It's a simple, traditional practice that brings calm and serenity into your bustling life and connects you to the essence of yoga.

8. Samadhi (Union)

Samadhi, the final limb of yoga, is often described as the ultimate goal, the grand culmination of the yogic journey. It's the state of complete absorption or oneness when you dive so deep into your practice that you become one with everything around you. It's a blissful connection where you realize your true self. Words struggle to capture the essence of Samadhi, as it's a deeply personal and transformative experience.

Reaching Samadhi is not a prerequisite for reaping the benefits of yoga. The true purpose of the eight limbs lies in the journey itself— the transformation we undergo as we cultivate ethical conduct, self-discipline, physical awareness, controlled breath, focused concentration, and effortless awareness. While Samadhi may seem like a distant peak, with consistent practice, we climb closer with each step, experiencing profound shifts in our perception of ourselves and the world around us.

Living Yoga: A Daily Practice of the Eight Limbs

Honoring the true essence of yoga transforms our day into a peaceful ritual where we move through each moment mindfully. Embracing the traditional eight limbs of yoga in our daily routine weaves ancient wisdom into our lives, enriching each day with the profound essence of inner peace. For the new generation, a holistic daily yoga practice rooted in tradition might look a little different, as mentioned below. This approach not only preserves the ancient wisdom of yoga but also adapts it to the dynamic lifestyles of the modern generation, promoting overall well-being and harmony.

Morning Rituals

Ahimsa (Non-Violence): Begin with positive thoughts or a kind gesture toward yourself or someone else. It could be a simple act of self-compassion, smiling at others, spreading warmth and kindness.

Saucha (Cleanliness): Approach your morning routine with mindfulness. Whether it's a refreshing shower or a quick face wash, focus on cleaning not just your body but also the spirit within.

Asana (Physical Postures): Start your day with gentle stretches or yoga poses. Focus on connecting your body with the calm of the morning.

Pranayama (Breath Control): Practice calming breathing exercises like Anulom Vilom (alternate nostril breathing) or deep breathing exercises, feeling each breath as a gift of life.

Afternoon Rituals

Santosha (Contentment): Nourishment extends beyond the food itself. Practice Santosha by savoring your lunch break. Turn off your phone, put away work emails, and focus on the present moment. Take slow, mindful bites, appreciating the texture, taste, and aroma of your meal. Give thanks for the sustenance it provides, recognizing the journey this food has taken to reach your plate. This practice of grateful eating fosters a sense of contentment and well-being.

Tapas (Discipline): The afternoon often finds us battling deadlines and juggling tasks. Here's where Tapas comes in. Approach your tasks with focus and dedication. Set realistic goals for yourself and dedicate focused effort to achieving them. Avoid distractions, and resist the urge to multitask. Each moment of disciplined effort becomes an offering to your higher self.

Ishvara Pranidhana (Surrender to the Divine): Sometimes, things don't go according to plan. Meetings run late, tasks take longer than expected, and unexpected challenges arise. This is where Ishvara Pranidhana becomes crucial. Take a moment to surrender to a higher purpose. Trust in the natural order of life, even when it feels chaotic. Release your grip on controlling outcomes and focus on what you can control – your attitude, your effort, and your response to situations.

Evening Rituals

Asteya (Non-Stealing): Asteya encourages us to be fully present in our interactions. When engaging in conversation, put away your phone, make eye contact, and truly listen to the person speaking. Offer your undivided attention as a sacred gift, avoiding the theft of presence.

Svadhyaya (Self-Study): Wind down with a meaningful reading or sacred texts that deepen your understanding of life's journey. This self-study nourishes your mind and spirit, offering new perspectives and insights.

Dharana (Concentration): During family time, put away distractions, silence the notifications, and turn off the TV. Fully focus on the simple joy of being together.

Night Rituals

Aparigraha (Non-Attachment): Before sleep, release the events of the day, letting go of worries, anxieties, and regrets. You cannot control the past, and the future remains uncertain. Detachment from worries allows you to drift off to sleep with a peaceful mind and a renewed sense of calm.

Pratyahara (Withdrawal of Senses): Dim the lights, put away electronic devices, and minimize external stimuli. The blue light emitted from screens can disrupt your sleep cycle, so disconnect at least an hour before bedtime. Allow your senses to settle, preparing your mind and body for a restful night's sleep.

Dhyana (Meditation): Spend a few moments in quiet meditation, allowing your mind to settle like a peaceful lake. Just be in the moment and experience the quiet.

Samadhi (State of Bliss): Take a moment to ponder the joyous moments in your day and your actions. Consider what you did well today for yourself and others and how you can improve tomorrow. When you engage in simple, thoughtful acts daily, you pave a path to Samadhi, a state of profound peace and unity. Through these small, meaningful actions, you can genuinely experience the tranquillity and togetherness that Samadhi offers.

As you explore the journey of poses and take those intentional breaths, remember that the essence of yoga extends beyond the mat. Here's to discovering your unique path toward a more meaningful and centered existence.

Chapter 7

Observing the Traditional Fasts

Fasting has a significant place in Hinduism. It offers a path toward spiritual connection, self-discipline, and inner peace. By avoiding specific foods or actions for a period, fasting symbolizes sacrifice and purification. It's a way to seek blessings, inner strength, and clarity.

Importance of Fasts in Today's Society

In today's fast-moving society, fasting retains its spiritual and personal importance. Amidst the hustle and bustle of modern life, people continue to use fasting to find inner peace, balance, and a spiritual connection. By denying ourselves physical pleasures for a period, we cultivate self-control and strengthen our resolve. Many integrate fasting into their contemporary routines to explore self-discipline, introspection, and a deeper understanding of their beliefs. It acts as a pause in our rapid lives, offering moments for reflection, mindfulness, and spiritual rejuvenation. It's a way to reconnect with ourselves and our values in a world that often prioritizes external stimuli. This chapter will explore the widely observed fasts in Hindu culture.

Ekadashi Fast

Ekadashi in the Hindu calendar occurs twice a month, on the 11th day after the Full Moon and the New Moon. These days are devoted to God Vishnu and involve fasting, prayer, and spiritual practices. People Worship God Vishnu, chant prayers, and engage in devotional activities.

The fast is observed for 24 hours, starting from the sunrise of the Ekadashi to the next morning. Some may observe a completely waterless fast, while others observe a modified fast that allows for fruits, nuts, dairy products, vegetables such as Karela (Bitter Lemon), Loki, Parmal, Okra (Lady Fingers), all leafy vegetables: Spinach, Salads, Cabbages, and Leafy Herbs, like Parsley, Curry Leaves, Neem Leaves, etc. The fast is ended after sunrise the next day, followed by prayers of gratitude to God Vishnu.

As with any religious practice, the specific rituals and dietary preferences might vary based on individual beliefs and traditions. Consulting elders or religious authorities for guidance is advisable, especially for newcomers to these practices.

Navratri Fast

Navratri, a vibrant Hindu festival that lasts nine nights and ten days, is observed a few times a year, each with unique significance. During Navratri, devotees worship the powerful Goddess Durga, seeking blessings for well-being and prosperity. Navratri details are covered in the Festival Section under Navratri, providing comprehensive information on this celebration. For further insights, refer to that section.

For those observing fasting during Navratri, the fast can range from complete abstinence from food to a simpler approach of consuming specific Navratri-friendly foods.

Food to Eat

- Fruits: All kinds of fruits are allowed.
- Vegetables: Potatoes, sweet potatoes, pumpkin, and bottle gourd are allowed.
- Grains: Specific grains like buckwheat, water chestnut flour, amaranth, and sama rice are allowed.
- Dairy: Milk, yogurt, paneer (cottage cheese), and buttermilk are allowed.

- Nuts and Seeds: Cashews, almonds, peanuts, and pumpkin seeds are allowed.
- Beverages: Water, coconut water, herbal teas, and fruit juices are common choices.

Food to avoid

- Grains: Wheat, rice, and other regular grains are avoided.
- Non-vegetarian Food: Meat, fish, and eggs are not consumed.
- Onions and Garlic: These ingredients are often avoided in fasting meals.
- Regular Salt: Regular salt is replaced by rock salt (sendha namak).

It's important to remember that fasting practices are a personal journey. There's no single "right" way to observe a fast. The key lies in finding an approach that resonates with you and supports your individual beliefs and traditions. If you're new to fasting, it's wise to start gradually, perhaps by observing a simple one-day fast or choosing a less restrictive approach. Listen to your body and prioritize your well-being throughout the process.

Maha Shivratri Fast

Maha Shivratri, literally translates to "The Great Night of Shiva," is a significant Hindu festival celebrated annually. The exact date of Maha Shivratri varies based on the Lunar calendar, typically falling in February or March. Devotees observe this occasion with fasting, prayers, and worship to honor God Shiva. The entire chapter dedicated to Maha Shivratri can be found in the festival section for your reference. Fasting practices during Maha Shivratri vary based on personal preferences and regional customs.

Food to Eat

- No Food/Water Fast: Some devotees choose to eat or drink nothing, while others opt for a water fast.
- Fruits: Many devotees consume fruits like bananas, apples, oranges, and melons during the fast.
- Milk and Dairy Products: Some may drink or consume milk, yogurt, and other dairy products.

Food to Avoid

- Grains and Cereals: Rice, wheat, lentils, and grains are avoided.
- Onions and Garlic: Aromatic vegetables like onions and garlic are avoided.

- Non-vegetarian Food: Meat, fish, and eggs are not consumed.
- Salt: Salt is not consumed during the fast.

It's important to remember that fasting practices are a personal journey. There's no single "right" way to observe a fast. The key lies in finding an approach that resonates with you and supports your individual beliefs and traditions.

It's advisable to consult with elders, religious leaders, or healthcare professionals for guidance, especially if health concerns or dietary restrictions must be considered during the fast.

Ahoy/ Ahoi Mata Fast

Ahoi Ashtami, also known as Ahoi Vrat, is a beautiful fast observed by mothers for the well-being and longevity of their sons. During Ahoi Ashtami, women observe a Nirjala fast and perform rituals in the evening to worship Ahoi Mata. According to the Hindu lunar calendar, it falls on the fourth day of the Krishna Paksha (the waning phase of the moon) in the month of Kartik, typically in October or November.

How to Observe Ahoi Ashtami Fast

- Begin the day with a cleansing bath, symbolizing both inner and outer purification.

- Set up the Altar with an Ahoi Mata picture or Calendar. Lovingly, write the names of all your children (sons) clearly on the picture or calendar provided. This serves as a dedicated offering in honor of their well-being. Ensure each name is written legibly and with reverence, reflecting the importance of this gesture in the ritual.

- Place a sacred 'Kalash' copper/silver water pot filled with water, adorned with a Swastik and a holy thread, next to an image of Ahoi Mata calendar.

- Observe the fast by abstaining from food and water until the stars appear in the night sky.

- Make Puris, Halwa, Chane, and sweets for the Puja in the Evening.

- Perform Ahoi Mata Puja before breaking the fast.

- Light a Lamp, burn incense, and ring the bell.

- Place offerings such as flowers, fruits, money, and food such as halwa, puri, boiled chana, and the children's favorite sweets in front of the Ahoi Mata picture.

- Engage in the storytelling of Ahoi Mata Katha, either by listening to an elderly woman or reading it yourself.

- Distribute sweets to family members after the puja.

- Conclude the fast by seeing the stars and celebrating with a vegetarian feast.

NOTE:

- Some families craft garlands from currency notes, adding them to the Ahoi Mata picture each year. This tradition is completed until the child's marriage or is handed down to descendants, adorned with additional notes.

- Many mothers observe a tradition of making anklets/ bracelets/ mala for their sons, which are made from cowrie shells, symbolizing protection and long life.

- Some mothers also create a Syahu Mala for their sons. This necklace includes a square silver locket depicting Syahu and her babies, along with silver beads that symbolize health, family growth, and prosperity. Blessed with intentions and prayers, the locket is placed in a Kalava (sacred thread). Each year, during the Ahoi Fast, mothers add a silver or gold bead to represent the child's age and to invoke blessings for his longevity. Traditionally, the necklace is passed from mother-in-law to daughter-in-law. However, in some families, it is reserved for special occasions such as a child's marriage or is handed down to children and future generations, enriched with wealth of silver and gold.

Ahoi Mata Katha/Story

Once, in a village near a dense forest, lived a kind and devoted woman. She had seven children. One day, with the intention of renovating her home, she ventured into the forest to gather clay soil. When she was digging the soil, she unknowingly hit a lion cub with her spade, which killed the cub. She felt remorseful for what happened.

Later in the same year, all her seven children disappeared. There was no trace of what happened to them. Villagers assumed that some wild animals may have killed them. Grief-stricken and wracked with guilt, she suspected a connection to her past deed. She shared her sorrow with wise old ladies of the village, and they advised her to worship the Goddess Ahoi, the incarnation of Goddess Parvati, and seek forgiveness for her sin. She was also advised to sketch the face of the cub she had killed while worshipping Ahoi Mata and observe fast.

The woman drew the cub's face and offered puja to Ahoi Mata with complete loyalty and devotion. Goddess Ahoi appeared before her and gave her the boon of long life to her sons. After that, all seven of her sons returned home alive. Since then, mothers have observed the tradition of Ahoi Ashtami, seeking the blessings of Ahoi Mata for the well-being and long life of their sons every year.

It's important to note that regional variations in traditions and customs may exist, and practices may differ in different communities. Consulting elders or religious authorities for guidance is advisable for beginners or those unfamiliar with the practices.

The Syahu Mala Story

A moneylender's youngest bride, while gathering mud for Diwali, accidentally killed seven porcupine babies and was cursed by the grieving porcupine mother to lose all her children. For seven years, each of her male children was taken by Syahu on Kartik Krishna Ashtami. In the eighth year, following advice to prepare a feast and win Syahu's favor, the bride laid out a grand spread and pinched her child to make him cry, claiming he wanted Syahu's earrings. Syahu, satisfied by the feast, gave up seven quills, restoring the bride's children.

Honoring and following the traditions set by our elders is important. By upholding these practices and showing reverence for the wisdom passed down through generations, we preserve the essence of our spiritual heritage and strengthen our connection to these meaningful traditions.

Karwa Chauth Fast

Karwa Chauth is a fasting ritual observed by married Hindu women around October or November. They fast from sunrise to moonrise for their husband's well-being and prosperity. The fast symbolizes love and devotion between spouses. For comprehensive details about Karwa Chauth fast, please refer to the festival chapter titled "Karwa Chauth."

Days Of the Week Fast

In Hinduism, specific days of the week are traditionally dedicated to particular deities and associated with fasting practices. Each day holds unique spiritual significance, believed to enhance devotion and deepen one's connection to the divine. Observing these fasts on their designated days can profoundly enrich spiritual practice and align practitioners with the divine attributes of each day.

Monday Fast (Somvar Vrat)

The Somvar Vrat, or Monday fasting, is observed to honor God Shiva, particularly on Mondays. Observing this fast is believed to please God Shiva and seek his blessings for a prosperous and fulfilling life. It is thought to remove obstacles, grant wishes, and bring happiness and marital bliss.

How to Observe Somvar Fast

- Devotees typically wake up early, take a ritual bath for purification, and visit Shiva temples to offer their prayers.
- Water, milk, flowers, and Bilva leaves are offered to the Shiva Linga, symbolizing their devotion and seeking the blessings of Lord Shiva.
- Fasting starts at sunrise and lasts until sunset; abstaining from food and sometimes water.
- Throughout the day, many devotees read or listen to Shiva Purana, chant mantras dedicated to God Shiva, and pray to deepen their spiritual connection.

Foods to Eat

- Fruits: Most fruits, such as bananas, apples, oranges, and melons, are permissible.
- Dairy Products: Milk, yogurt, and paneer (cottage cheese) are commonly consumed.
- Nuts and Dry Fruits: Almonds, cashews, raisins, and other nuts are allowed.
- Non-grain Flours: Dishes made from non-grain flours like singhare ka atta (water chestnut flour) or kuttu ka atta (buckwheat flour) are often consumed.

Foods to Avoid

- Grains and Lentils: Rice, wheat, lentils, and other grains are usually avoided.
- Onions and Garlic: Pungent vegetables like onions and garlic are avoided.
- Non-Vegetarian Food: Non-vegetarian items are not consumed during the fast.

Observing Somvar Vrat is considered highly auspicious. It promotes devotion and seeks blessings from God Shiva for spiritual growth and fulfillment of desires. The specific rituals and practices might vary based on personal beliefs and traditions. Consulting elders or religious authorities for guidance is advisable for beginners or those unfamiliar with the practices.

Tuesday Fast (Mangalvar Vrat)

Devotees observe the Tuesday fast to seek the blessings and protection of Lord Hanuman, revered for his unwavering devotion, formidable strength, and unparalleled dedication.

How to Observe Tuesday Fast (Mangalvar Vrat)

- Devotees wake up early, perform a ritual bath, and either visit Hanuman temples or conduct prayers at home.
- Offerings of red flowers, vermilion (sindoor), and sweets are made to Lord Hanuman.
- Reading Hanuman Chalisa or scriptures dedicated to Hanuman is a customary practice.
- Wearing attire in shades of red, symbolizing the planet Mars, is considered auspicious on Tuesdays.

Foods to Eat

- Fruits: Most fruits, such as bananas, apples, oranges, and melons, are permissible.
- Dairy Products: Milk, yogurt, and paneer (cottage cheese) are commonly consumed.

- Nuts and Dry Fruits: Almonds, cashews, raisins, and other nuts are allowed.

- Non-grain Flours: Dishes made from non-grain flours like singhare ka atta (water chestnut flour) or kuttu ka atta (buckwheat flour) are often consumed.

Foods to Avoid

- Grains and Lentils: Rice, wheat, lentils, and other grains are usually avoided.

- Onions and Garlic: Pungent vegetables like onions and garlic are avoided.

- Non-Vegetarian Food: Non-vegetarian items are refrained from during the fast.

Maintaining simplicity in meals and focusing on easily digestible and pure foods are essential while observing the Mangalvar fast dedicated to God Hanuman. The specific food choices might differ based on individual preferences and regional customs. Consulting elders or religious leaders for guidance is advisable, especially if there are dietary restrictions or health concerns.

Wednesday Fast (Budhvar Vrat)

Wednesday, known as Budhvar in Hindi, is associated with the God Vishnu, Lord Krishna, and the planet Mercury (Budha Graha). Fasting on Wednesdays is believed to invoke blessings for wisdom, knowledge, effective— communication, and success.

How to Observe Wednesday Fast (Budhvar Vrat)

- Devotees rise early, perform a ritual bath, and either visit Vishnu temples or conduct prayers at home.
- Offerings of water, milk, and Tulsi leaves (holy basil) are presented to God Vishnu.
- Reciting Vishnu Sahasranama (thousand names of God Vishnu) or other Vishnu-related prayers is common.
- Wearing attire in shades of yellow or offering yellow flowers is considered auspicious, as yellow represents the planet Mercury.

Foods to Eat

- Fruits: Bananas, apples, oranges, and melons are allowed.
- Dairy Products: Milk, yogurt, and paneer (cottage cheese) are commonly consumed.

- Nuts and Dry Fruits: Almonds, cashews, raisins, and other nuts are allowed.
- Non-grain Flours: Dishes made from non-grain flours like singhare ka atta (water chestnut flour) or kuttu ka atta (buckwheat flour) are often consumed.

Foods to Avoid

- Grains and Lentils: Rice, wheat, lentils, and other grains are usually avoided.
- Onions and Garlic: Pungent vegetables like onions and garlic are omitted.
- Non-Vegetarian Food: Non-vegetarian items are not consumed during the fast.

The Wednesday fast is observed with reverence and is believed to bestow wisdom, knowledge, success, and overall well-being. As with any religious practice, specific rituals and dietary preferences may vary based on individual beliefs and traditions. Seeking guidance from elders or religious authorities is advisable, especially for newcomers to these practices.

Thursday Fast (Guruvar Vrat)

Devotees observe the Thursday fast to seek the blessings and guidance of Lord Brihaspati, who embodies wisdom, learning, and good fortune.

How to Observe Thursday Fast (Guruvar Vrat)

- Devotees rise early, perform a ritual bath, and either visit Jupiter (Brihaspati) temples or conduct prayers at home.
- Offerings of water, yellow flowers, and gram lentils (chana dal) are made to Lord Brihaspati.
- Recitation of the Guru Mantra or Brihaspati Stotram (prayers dedicated to Lord Brihaspati) is customary.

Foods to Eat

- Fruits: Most fruits are permissible, including bananas, apples, oranges, and melons.
- Dairy Products: Milk, yogurt, and paneer (cottage cheese) are consumed.
- Nuts and Dry Fruits: Almonds, cashews, raisins, and other nuts are allowed.

- Non-grain Flours: Dishes made from non-grain flours, such as singhara ka atta (water chestnut flour) or kuttu ka atta (buckwheat flour), are often included.

Foods to Avoid

- Grains and Lentils: Rice, wheat, lentils, and other grains are typically avoided.
- Onions and Garlic: Pungent vegetables like onions and garlic are omitted.
- Non-Vegetarian Food: Non-vegetarian items are refrained from during the fast.

The Thursday fast dedicated to Lord Brihaspati is observed with utmost devotion and is believed to bring knowledge, success, prosperity, and overall well-being. As with any religious practice, specific rituals and dietary preferences may vary based on individual beliefs and traditions. Seeking guidance from elders or religious authorities is advisable, especially for newcomers to these practices.

Friday Fast (Shukravar Vrat)

Friday, known as Shukravar in Hindi, is associated with Goddess Lakshmi, the radiant deity of wealth, prosperity, and fortune. Observing fasts on Fridays is believed to appease Goddess Lakshmi and seek her blessings for a life filled with abundance, prosperity, and happiness.

How to Observe Friday Fast (Shukravar Vrat)

- Devotees wake up early, take a ritual bath, visit Lakshmi temples, or perform prayers at home to offer prayers and participate in devotional ceremonies.
- Offerings of water, sweets, and lotus flowers are presented to Goddess Lakshmi.
- Reciting Lakshmi Mantra or singing devotional songs dedicated to Goddess Lakshmi is a common practice throughout the day.

Foods to Eat

- Fruits: Most fruits like bananas, apples, oranges, and melons are allowed.
- Dairy Products: Milk, yogurt, and paneer (cottage cheese) are consumed.

- Nuts and Dry Fruits: Almonds, cashews, raisins, and other nuts are allowed.

- Non-grain Flours: Dishes made from non-grain flours like singhare ka atta (water chestnut flour) or kuttu ka atta (buckwheat flour) are often chosen as alternatives to traditional grains.

Foods to Avoid

- Grains and Lentils: Rice, wheat, lentils, and other grains are typically avoided during the fast.

- Onions and Garlic: People avoid using pungent vegetables like onions and garlic to maintain a sense of purity.

- Non-Vegetarian Food: Non-vegetarian items are not consumed during the fast.

The Friday fast dedicated to Goddess Lakshmi is observed with devotion and is believed to bring wealth, prosperity, and overall well-being. As with any religious practice, specific rituals and dietary preferences might vary based on individual beliefs and traditions. Seeking guidance from elders or religious authorities is advisable, especially for newcomers to these practices.

Saturday Fast (Shanivar Vrat)

Saturday, known as Shanivar in Hindi, is associated with God Shani (Saturn), the deity who governs discipline, Karma, and life lessons.

Devotees observe the Saturday fast to seek blessings and relief from hardships, protection from negative influences, and the strength to overcome challenges.

How to Observe Saturday Fast (Shanivar Vrat)

- Devotees wake up early, take a ritual bath, and visit Lord Shani temples or perform prayers at home.
- Offerings of sesame oil, black sesame seeds, black cloth, and black gram lentils (urad dal) – all symbolic of Shani Dev – are presented.
- Reciting Shani Mantras or Shani Stotram (prayers dedicated to Lord Shani) is a common practice.
- Wearing black attire or offering black flowers is considered auspicious.

Foods to Eat

- Fruits: Most fruits, such as bananas, apples, oranges, and melons, are permissible.

- Dairy Products: Milk, yogurt, and paneer (cottage cheese) are consumed.

- Nuts and Dry Fruits: Almonds, cashews, raisins, and other nuts are allowed.

- Non-grain Flours: Dishes made from non-grain flours like singhare ka atta (water chestnut flour) or kuttu ka atta (buckwheat flour) are often consumed.

Foods to Avoid

- Grains and Lentils: Rice, wheat, lentils, and other grains are usually avoided.

- Onions and Garlic: These pungent vegetables are excluded.

- Non-Vegetarian Food: Non-vegetarian items are not consumed during the fast.

The Saturday fast dedicated to God Shani is observed with devotion and is believed to bring relief from hardships, protection from negative influences, and overall well-being. Specific rituals and dietary preferences might vary based on individual beliefs and traditions. Seeking guidance from elders or religious authorities is advisable, especially for newcomers to these practices.

Sunday Fast (Ravivar Vrat)

In contrast to Friday and Saturday, specific fasting rituals dedicated to Sundays (Ravivar) are less prevalent in Hinduism. However, some individuals may observe fasts or perform spiritual practices on Sundays for personal reasons or in reverence to the Sun God (Surya Deva).

Foods to Eat

- Fruits: Most fruits, such as bananas, apples, oranges, and melons, are permissible.
- Dairy Products: Milk, yogurt, and paneer (cottage cheese) are commonly consumed.
- Nuts and Dry Fruits: Almonds, cashews, raisins, and other nuts are allowed.
- Non-grain Flours: Dishes made from non-grain flours like singhare ka atta (water chestnut flour) or kuttu ka atta (buckwheat flour) are often consumed.

Foods to Avoid

- Grains and Lentils: Rice, wheat, lentils, and other grains are avoided.

- Onions and Garlic: Pungent vegetables like onions and garlic are avoided.
- Non-Vegetarian Food: Non-vegetarian items are not consumed.

While the food restrictions are important, the true essence of these weekday fasts lies in their spiritual significance. Fasting serves as a form of self-discipline, a way to cleanse the body and mind and to focus one's devotion on the respective deity. The practices associated with each fast—from prayers and offerings to mantras and hymns—further deepen the connection with the divine.

Chapter 8

Celebrating Festivals of Hinduism

Hindu festivals are vibrant and joyful celebrations filled with color, devotion, and tradition. They hold deep spiritual meaning and reflect the rich cultural heritage of Hinduism. These festivals are not just times of joy but also important expressions of faith and community. They follow the natural cycles, commemorate historical events, and honor divine beings. By exploring Hindu festivals, we can better understand Hinduism, a religion that connects the earthly with the divine, the individual with the universal, and the past with the present. This chapter will take you through major celebrated festivals, explaining their rituals, stories, and why they are still important today.

Lohri

The Festival Calendar

The word "Lohri" is thought to come from "loh" (iron) and "ari" (saw), signifying the tools used for the harvest. Another popular explanation points to "Tilohri," where "til" (sesame) and "rorhi" (jaggery) play a special role. Sesame and jaggery are believed to purify the body and bring fresh energy to life. Celebrated on January 13th in regular calendars, Lohri marks the end of harsh winter and welcomes the promise of spring with open arms. In the Hindu calendar, Lohri is celebrated just before Makar Sankranti, spreading warmth and joy.

The Festival Stories

Lohri is a happy and lively festival with fascinating stories. These stories reflect the cultural diversity, shared joy, and special meaning that make Lohri a cherished celebration in our hearts and homes.

Since Ancient times, people have been lighting a fire and chanting to the Sun God, Surya and it was believed that Flames of Fire took their message to the Sun God for bringing warmth and taking away the cold weather. In old times, humans also lit fires to keep away flesh-eating animals and protect their habitat. The whole village contributed to communal fire. The Lohri has been associated with fire worship. People gather around crackling bonfires, chanting hymns in reverence to the Sun God. This ancient tradition signifies the vanquishing of the harsh winter chill and the yearning for the nurturing sun's rays.

A popular legend also states a story about a king named Hiranyakashyap who desired to be worshipped as a God by everyone. However, his son Prahalad remained devoted to God Vishnu, refusing to worship his father. This defiance angered the king deeply.

Hiranyakashyap tried many times to harm Prahalad, but nothing worked. Finally, he ordered one of his sisters, Holika, who had a special cloak protecting her from fire, to take Prahalad into the flames. But something miraculously happened! As the fire blazed, the cloak flew from Holika to Prahalad, saving him.

Witnessing this miracle, another sister, Lohri, aided Prahalad in getting him out of the fire. Enraged by these failures, Hiranyakashyap decided to take matters into his own hands. He tied Prahalad and threatened to kill him, challenging him to call upon God Vishnu for help.

Undeterred, Prahalad closed his eyes and fervently prayed to Vishnu. Answering his devotee's call, Vishnu appeared in the formidable form of Narasimha, swiftly defeating Hiranyakashyap and ending his tyranny. This tale illustrates the power of faith and divine intervention.

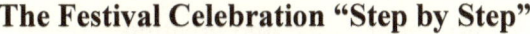

According to the cultural history of Punjab, Lohri is also associated with weddings. Legends weave tales of Dulla Bhatti, a charismatic figure often compared to Robinhood. He fearlessly fought against injustice, robbing the rich and distributing wealth among the poor. People loved and respected him. One of his noble deeds involved rescuing young girls from being sold on the slave market. He helped arrange marriages for them and provided their dowries. Two girls he helped were Sunder and Munder. They became part of the folklore. His story reminds men about the braveness, large-heartedness, and sincerity of the great heroism of a man.

The Festival Celebration "Step by Step"

Even in the West, far from its Indian roots, families come together to keep and spread Lohri's essence through time-honoured rituals, embracing togetherness, and savouring festive flavours.

The first Lohri after a son's wedding or the birth of a baby boy is a momentous occasion in Hindu culture, brimming with joy and significance. A son's wedding represents not just a union of two individuals but the expansion of the family, making it a cherished celebration of growth and togetherness. Likewise, the arrival of a newborn son is a precious blessing, igniting hearts with boundless happiness and anticipation for the future. In Hindu tradition, both milestones are celebrated with grandeur and warmth as family and friends gather to mark the auspicious moments with joyous festivities and heartfelt blessings. Let's celebrate Lohri with easy yet meaningful steps.

Prepare for the Festival

Begin by cleaning your home and creating a fresh and welcoming space for the festivities. Dress yourselves in comfortable yet traditional attire.

Offer Morning Prayers to the Sun

Begin the day by offering water mixed with rice, tika/turmeric, and flowers to the Sun, symbolizing gratitude and respect for its life-giving energy. You may also start the day with Sun Salutations through yoga, connecting with the Sun's vitality and radiance as you embark on the festivities.

Perform Vishnu/Narayan Puja

Perform a puja dedicated to God Vishnu/Narayan, following the sacred rituals outlined in the Puja chapter "How to Perform Puja," taking the time to understand the meaning and purpose behind each ritual. This awareness enhances your connection with the divine and enriches your spiritual experience. If time is limited, follow the steps of "A Simple Daily Puja" with a simple prayer as described under "Puja and Prayer Methods." Offer heartfelt prayers to God Vishnu, expressing gratitude and devotion and seeking blessings for spiritual fulfillment and guidance in life's journey.

Spread Kindness and Donate Generously

Remember Dulla Bhatti's legendary generosity. Consider donating food, clothes, or money to a charity or to the homeless that aligns with Lohri's values of helping those in need.

Create a Cozy Evening Bonfire

Extend the joy by inviting your loved ones to join the festivities, fostering a sense of togetherness. Set up a bonfire in your backyard, create a cozy atmosphere with a fireplace indoors, or join the fun in the temple. The flickering flames become a focal point for gathering, sharing stories, and basking in the warmth.

Offer Prayers

Pray and offer sesame seeds/til, daikon, and sugarcane to the fire. This tradition symbolizes prosperity, purification, and protection. It's believed to dispel negativity and evil spirits. As you offer sadness, fear, and laziness, you welcome happiness, freshness, and prosperity into your life.

Infuse the Energy

Add rhythm to the celebration by singing traditional songs and dancing. Don't forget the Dulla Bhatti song; its lively rhythm adds fun and energy. As you dance and sing, create a vibrant atmosphere that celebrates the spirit of Lohri.

In India, particularly Punjab, Lohri features a heartwarming tradition: children going door-to-door collecting treats for Lohri in honor of Dulla Bhatti. People then give money and sweets to the kids. Groups of children move from door to door, singing:

Sunder mundriye – ho!	Tera kaun vicharaa – ho!
Dullah Bhatti walla – ho!	Dullhe di dhee vyayae – ho!
Ser shakkar payee – ho!	Kudi da saalu paata – ho!
Salu kaun samete – ho!	Chacha choori kutte – ho!
Zamindar Bulaye- ho!	Gin Gin Bhole Laye – ho!

Eka bhola ghat gaya, Zamindar nas gaya.

Sade pera heth rod, sanu jaldi tor.

Sanoo de de Lohri, teri jeeve jodi.

This song celebrates Dulla Bhatti's bravery, praising him for rescuing girls and arranging their marriages with gifts. His heroic deeds and compassion are highlighted, and through this song, his legacy is remembered and honored.

Incorporating the Dulla Bhatti song into your Lohri celebrations adds a fun element and creates a vibrant and inclusive atmosphere. Singing and dancing together allows everyone, regardless of age or background, to truly partake in the joy of Lohri and create lasting memories.

Indulge in Delightful Treats

No celebration is complete without delightful treats. Indulge in the quintessential flavours of Lohri – revitalizing sesame seed sweets (Rewari), crunchy peanuts, melt-in-your-mouth Gachak (a sweet and savory deep-fried snack), the unique taste of Bhugga and the refreshing sweetness of sugarcane.

Capture Warmth Through Photographs

Preserve the warmth and togetherness of these special family moments by clicking photographs, creating a beautiful visual diary of the celebration.

The Lohri Celebration for a Son's Wedding and Birth of a Son

During the first Lohri, after a son's marriage, families share traditional sweets like bhugga, Rewari, gachaks, and peanuts with neighbours, friends, and relatives. This act, called giving Lohri, represents joy and prosperity, making the occasion more festive. Inviting loved ones to celebrate the first Lohri at home fosters a sense of togetherness and community, as everyone comes together to mark these important moments in the family's life.

Relatives and friends gather to offer gifts, sweets, and best wishes to the newlyweds, strengthening family bonds and community connections. This celebration marks the start of a new journey for the couple and embodies love, happiness, and togetherness.

In the cherished tradition of celebrating a son's birth during Lohri, families gather around bonfires to perform sacred rituals. The newborn baby is warmly welcomed, and heartfelt prayers are said for his health, happiness, and prosperity. Relatives and friends shower blessings, gifts, and sweets upon the child and his family, marking this occasion with deep cultural significance. It symbolizes the continuation of the family lineage and is believed to bring good fortune to the household.

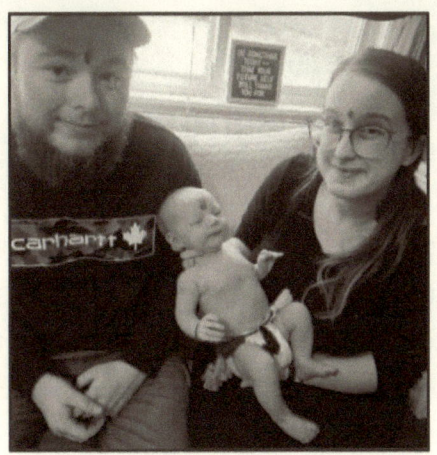

After the festivities, the joyous atmosphere continues as families and friends gather for a sumptuous feast filled with delectable dishes and flavours. Laughter fills the air as lively music sets the stage for singing and dancing, with everyone celebrating the occasion with exuberance and merriment.

The Festival Legacy

Lohri is more than just a festival; it's about creating a cherished family legacy. Lohri involves engaging every family member, young and old. By passing down the stories and songs associated with Lohri, we foster continuity, a sense of belonging, and a celebration resonating with love, laughter, and cultural richness.

Holi

The Festival Calendar

Holi, named after Holika, rejoices in the triumph of good over evil. Holi arrives in February-March (English) or the full moon of Phalgun (Hindu), welcoming the lively spirit of spring. Celebrated with colorful festivities, Holi symbolizes the victory of brightness over winter's darkness. It unites people, breaking barriers with playful colors.

The Festival Stories

Holi, the vibrant festival of colors, is steeped in rich cultural tales that contribute to its diverse origins. Let's uncover the various stories that shape Holi's essence and the joyous spirit it brings.

Once upon a time, there was a king named Hiranyakashyap. Blessed with boons from the mighty God Shiva, he believed himself invincible, impervious to harm from any human or deity, in day nor night, indoors nor outdoors, inland, in air or water, and by animate or inanimate weapons.

However, consumed by a thirst for power, Hiranyakashyap demanded that everyone worship him, elevating himself above the Gods. However, his son Prahlad refused to obey his orders and continued his faith in God Vishnu. Despite many efforts, Prahlad declined to consider his father a God. The king's power knew no bounds, leading him to plot the demise of his son, Prahlad, employing various means.

Despite the king's relentless efforts to harm Prahlad, the divine protection of God Vishnu shielded him unfailingly. In a final desperate bid, the king's sister, Holika, endowed with the ability to withstand fire, sought to save herself by attempting to burn Prahlad alive. Yet, her power could only be activated if she entered the flames wearing a cloak. Tragically, her fatal mistake cost her life, while Prahlad, unwavering in his devotion to Vishnu, remained unscathed as the cloak flew from Holika to him, sparing him from the flames.

Enraged by his son's unyielding faith, the king resorted to chaining Prahlad to a pillar, daring him to summon his protector, God Vishnu. Responding to the call of his devotee, Vishnu emerged from within the pillar in the form of Narasimha, swiftly putting an end to the tyrant king's life. Despite the king's invincibility, he met his demise at the hands of Narasimha, neither human nor animal, as dusk fell at the doorstep, succumbing to the claws of divine justice.

This story of good winning over evil gave birth to Holi. It teaches us that true faith, like Prahlad's, is always protected, and those who try to harm the faithful will lose.

卐

Holi, in addition, holds special significance as a festival dedicated to Lord Krishna. It commemorates an intriguing tale from Krishna's childhood involving the demoness Putna. Legend has it that Putna, a formidable demoness, sought to eliminate the infant Krishna by feeding him poisoned milk. However, Krishna, in his divine wisdom, turned the tables on Putna, and she met her demise at his hands.

As Krishna suckled from her, he absorbed the poison, which turned his complexion into a deep blue hue.

Curious about this change in his appearance, young Krishna questioned his mother about it, wondering why he appeared darker while his beloved Radha possessed a fair complexion. Following his mother's advice, Krishna playfully applied color to Radha, and soon, their friends joined in, covering each other in vibrant hues. This act unified their appearances, fostering a sense of equality and companionship among them.

Since that eventful day, people have continued the tradition of applying colors to each other during Holi, symbolizing breaking down barriers and celebrating unity in diversity.

卐

During the vibrant festival of Holi, we are also reminded of the divine tale of God Shiva and Kamadeva. Shiva, the tranquil yogi immersed in meditation, was interrupted by Kamadeva's attempt to stir love within him. Despite Shiva's preference for solitude and spiritual devotion, Kamadeva, wielding his love arrows, sought to awaken emotions of love in the serene deity.

Shiva's third eye blazed open in a moment of divine fury, reducing Kamadeva to ashes. Yet, in the aftermath of this fiery spectacle, the power of compassion prevailed. Moved by Kamadeva's sacrifice and the pleas of his grieving wife, Shiva, the embodiment of mercy, restored Kamadeva to life.

This enchanting saga encapsulates profound wisdom, emphasizing that while worldly desires may entice, true fulfillment blossoms from inner peace and spiritual evolution. In the dance of existence, where love and solitude intertwine, the grace of Shiva's compassion illuminates the path to transcendence.

The Festival Celebration "Step by Step"

During Holi, people reenact Holika's burning to signify good triumphing over evil. Some throw cow dung into the fire, shouting at Holika, 'Holi-hai! Holi-hai!' The festival starts with a bonfire on the first day to dispel winter's darkness. On the second day, colorful festivities begin with water, colors, and balloons, making it India's most vibrant and fun-filled celebration.

Holi Shopping List

1. Besan (gram flour)
2. Turmeric powder
3. Dry organic colors
4. Flowers for adornment
5. Wet colors
6. Mustard oil or Ghee for Diya
7. Flour dough (for Diyas) 2 sided and 4 sided
8. Materials for Rangoli
9. Unrefined thread/Kacha soot/Dhaga (if available)

Holika Day (Day 1)

This day is significant and signifies the victory of good over evil. While some devotees conduct intricate Puja ceremonies, here are some simple steps you can follow.

- Mix Besan flour and turmeric, and apply the paste to your face and body. Once it almost dries, remove the paste and place it on a piece of paper. Later, during the Holika bonfire, Facing Northeast, offer this paste to Holika, symbolizing the release of negativity and illness from your being.
- Participate in community/temple events and join the sacred ritual of burning Holika (done at night).
- Light, a four-sided flour dough Diya to Holika fire with mustard Oil. This represents illuminating four essential virtues: knowledge, righteousness, strength, and devotion.
- Tie or offer raw thread (kacha dhaga), if available, around the wood in the fire. The "kacha dhaga" (raw thread) used in tying

Holika Dahan symbolizes the binding of evil forces. As you do so, seek blessings and chant "Om Narsimhaya Namah."

- Afterward, perform seven parikramas (circumambulations) clockwise around the fire while continuing to seek blessings. In Hindu tradition, performing seven circles symbolizes completeness, cosmic alignment, and devotion to the divine, embodying a journey of spiritual fulfillment and reverence.

- Collect some ashes from the burnt Holika fire. You can either bring them home that night or the following morning. Ashes can be used for several purposes.

- Keep these ashes inside your home in a red cloth in a hidden area like a vault or with some money and Lakshmi Yantra for abundance.

- Hang or Hide ashes in a black cloth outside your home so that no negative energies can enter your home.

- Use ashes to take a ceremonial shower to remove all sickness or diseases from your body and mind.

- Apply Ash Tilak on your forehead, throat, chest, and belly to remove negative energies from your body.

Holi Day (Day 2)

During the next day of Holi, rituals range from traditional puja to playful color smearing, symbolizing devotion, renewal, unity, and joy.

Prepare and Decorate the Home

- Clean and decorate your home in the spirit of Holi. Craft a Rangoli in front of your home. Remember to incorporate Gulal (Pink Color) along with other hues.
- Light a Mustard Oil or Ghee 2-sided diya fashioned from flour dough, facing north alongside the Rangoli. The two-sided diya symbolizes the balance between light and darkness, reminding us to strive for enlightenment amidst life's dualities.

Perform Traditional Puja

Perform traditional Puja and follow the steps of "How to Perform Puja," as outlined in the Puja chapter, taking the time to understand the meaning and purpose behind each ritual. If time is limited, follow the steps of "A Simple Daily Puja" with a simple prayer as described under "Puja and Prayer Methods."

Play Holi with the Divine

Initiate the celebration of Holi by offering and applying God Shiva water in a copper lota infused with sandalwood paste. For Krishna and Radha, starting with the application of the following:

1. dry organic colors
2. flowers
3. wet colors
4. prayers

Engage in Hues of Holi

Explore and participate in the Holi celebrations in your home, local community centers, and cultural organizations.

- Gather Organic, vibrant-colored powders or watercolors.
- Dress in traditional attire.
- Invite friends and family for a joyful get-together.
- Play Holi tunes and add lively music to the celebration.
- Engage in a colorful paint war in the backyard in an open community area or at your local temple.
- After the fun, clean up and share warm wishes, fostering a sense of togetherness and joy.

- Enjoy delicious traditional Holi snacks or a delicious meal.
- Freeze time with your camera lens, preserving the magic of family unity and celebratory joy.
- End the day by ritually bathing the deities, symbolizing purity and renewal.

NOTE: Before immersing yourself fully in the colorful revelry of Holi, ensure your skin is protected by applying coconut oil, almond oil, sunscreen, and Vaseline to your face and body. This protective layer will facilitate the easy removal of colors afterward. Post-celebration, cleanse your skin effortlessly using lotion, water, and cotton to remove any remnants of the vibrant hues.

With its hues and happiness, Holi marks another beautiful chapter in the book of traditions, promising to return with more joy next year.

The Festival Legacy

Carrying on the age-old Holi traditions is crucial as it keeps us tied to our heritage, uniting families through colorful celebrations and joy. These customs connect us to our past, welcoming spring with love and togetherness. Passing down these cherished practices ensures the spirit of Holi lives on for our children and their children.

Maha Shivratri

The Festival Calendar

Maha Shivratri is a significant Hindu festival that is a night steeped in devotion, vibrant rituals, and captivating stories. "Maha" means "great," and "Shivratri" translates to "the night of Shiva." Thus, Maha Shivratri signifies the "great night of Shiva." Maha Shivratri falls in February or March in the English calendar and the 14th day in the dark fortnight of the month of Phalguna in the Indian Lunar Calendar.

The Festival Stories

As per Shiva Purana, the main story of Maha Shivratri is that once, God Brahma and God Vishnu debated about who was supreme. Suddenly, a massive pillar of light appeared, its top and bottom beyond sight. To find its limits, Brahma flew upwards as a swan while Vishnu burrowed downwards as a boar. Despite searching for ages, neither could find the end. Brahma, unable to find the top, encountered a Ketaki flower and convinced it to lie that he had reached the top. Upon returning, Brahma falsely claimed success, while Vishnu honestly admitted his failure.

At that moment, God Shiva emerged from the pillar of light, revealing himself as the infinite, formless, and supreme power. This divine revelation marked the first time God Shiva manifested himself in the form of a Linga, symbolizing his boundless and transcendent nature. He exposed Brahma's deceit and cursed him, declaring that Brahma would no longer be worshipped and forbidding the Ketaki flower in his worship.

This event marked the first manifestation of Shiva as a Linga, symbolizing his infinite nature. Celebrated as Maha Shivratri, this festival reminds us of Supreme God Shiva's boundless power, the importance of honesty, and the unity of divine forces.

The Festival Celebration "Step by Step"

Maha Shivratri, a sacred celebration for God Shiva, brings moments of devotion and joy. As devotees dress up, visit temples, and engage in rituals, the air is filled with prayers and reverence. This profound occasion is a time for spiritual connection, reflection, and expressing happiness through heartfelt traditions.

A simple Puja or rituals-filled Puja honors the divine, emphasizing that any Puja, when approached with sincere reverence, is truly meaningful and cherished.

You can simply follow the steps of "How to Perform Puja," as outlined in the Puja chapter, taking the time to understand the meaning and purpose behind each ritual. If time is limited, follow the steps of "A Simple Daily Puja" with a simple prayer as described under "Puja and Prayer Methods." As you progress on your spiritual journey, gradually incorporate one or all of the rituals specific to the festival.

Whether you're just starting or have been celebrating for years, the essence of these festivals lies in the devotion with which they are observed.

Maha Shivratri Checklist

1. Puja Thali with all required items (please see the Puja Chapter for details)
2. Water in copper/silver lota (bowl)
3. Rudraksha Mala
4. Mustard Oil
5. Tilak/Tika: Bhasam/Chandan/Sandalwood powder
6. 108 Long Grain Unbroken Rice (Prepared a day before)
7. Panchamrit offering in a Bowl (See Below for the ingredients)
8. 7 White Flowers
9. 2 Janews (threads) (if available)
10. Sugarcane Juice (if available)
11. 5 Fruits, including fruit Ber (if available)
12. 7 Bhel Patra (leaves) (if available)
13. 1 Dhatura (if available)

Optionally, you can prepare one or all these symbolic ingredients (per person) as an offering to the divine, each imbued with profound meanings.

- 1 Clove, 1 Black Pepper, and 7 Sesame Seeds in a bowl: Offering these Purifies one's intentions and protects one's well-being.

- 1 Cardamom and 1 Clove: Offering these signifies the divine union of Shiva and Shakti.

- 3 Paan leaves and Supari: Offering these present offering vices and bad habits to God Shiva to purify the mind and soul.

- 21 Wheat grains: Offering these blesses the devotee for abundance and nourishment.

- 7 Lotus Buds (Kamal Gatte): Offering these symbolizes love and beauty and evokes divine blessings and grace.

- 1 Ittar (Perfume): Offering this Infuses the atmosphere with divine fragrance and devotion, enhancing the sacred ambiance of the puja.

- Lentils (Masar, yellow, green moong): Offering these symbolizes passion, debt removal, prosperity, and growth in one's life.

- 21 Peppercorn: Offering these signifies purification and protection from negative energies.

Each ingredient adds depth and significance to your puja, fostering a deeper connection with the divine and inviting blessings into your life.

သ

The Day Before Maha Shivratri

- Gather the necessary ingredients and discover events in the community and temples.
- Ensure a light vegetarian meal in the evening, around 6 pm, if fasting for the festival.
- Perform the ritual in devotion to Shiva to manifest your heartfelt desires. This ritual is simple and can be done by anyone.

The Ritual to Manifest Desire

Ingredients

- 108 Long-grain unbroken rice (preferably Basmati or any other variety)
- Clean water for washing the rice
- Clean silver or copper bowl for the rice
- A quiet, sacred space for performing the ritual

Instructions:

1. Begin by showering and preparing the sacred space where you will perform the ritual. Ensure it is clean and free from distractions.
2. Wash the rice thoroughly under running water to cleanse them physically and symbolically.
3. Sit comfortably in front of your altar or sacred space, where you have placed the bowl for the rice.

4. Transfer 108 Grains of Rice to your left hand.

5. With your right hand, use your thumb and ring finger to pick up one grain of rice at a time from the pile in your left hand.

6. As you transfer each grain of rice to the bowl, offer a heartfelt prayer or desire to God Shiva. This could be a wish for spiritual growth, inner peace, prosperity, or personal desire.

7. Repeat this process of picking up one grain of rice at a time with your right hand and offering your prayer until you have placed 108 rice grains in the bowl.

8. Throughout the ritual, concentrate on offering your prayer to God Shiva. Visualize your desires manifesting with Shiva's blessings.

9. Once you have offered all 108 grains of rice and expressed your desires, close your eyes and take a moment to sit in silence, feeling the presence of God Shiva and the energy of your prayers.

10. Conclude the ritual with three reverberating claps, signifying the awakening of divine energy.

11. Use these rice grains as an offering to God Shiva in your home or temple during the auspicious occasion of Maha Shivratri, symbolizing your devotion and surrender to the divine.

12. After completing the ritual, remember to spray a couple of drops of water under your seat and gently touch this consecrated water to your forehead as a symbol of purification and divine connection.

The Day of Maha Shivratri

Start your day by getting up early in Brahmmahurat before sunrise. The best time is between 3 am and 5.30 am. Clean, Shower, and wear traditional, comfortable clothes. Set a strong intention for the day and ask for divine blessings. Fasting shall have been started the night before. Observe a complete or modified fast with fruits, water, and milk, honoring this auspicious day. Remember to refrain from consuming anything else during this time. Fast is broken the next day of Maha Shivratri by going to Shiva Temple or home temple and taking prasad and blessings from the temple.

Prepare Panchamrit

Panchamrit is a sacred elixir used in Hindu rituals. The name is derived from the Sanskrit words "Panch," meaning five, and "Amrit," meaning nectar of immortality. Panchamrit consists of five ingredients: milk, yogurt, honey, ghee, and sugar. Drinking Panchamrit after offering to the Deity is believed to purify the devotees and bring them closer to the divine.

॥ॐ॥

Ingredients

- 1 tablespoon Ghee (Clarified butter)
- 2 tablespoons Honey
- 4 tablespoons (Rock Sugar)
- 8 tablespoons Yogurt (Curd)
- 16 tablespoons Milk

Instructions:

Please note that these ingredients can be mixed together or offered to the -deity one by one, symbolizing the individual qualities and blessings each component brings.

Visit the Sacred Temples

On the day/evening/night of Maha Shivratri, visit temples dedicated to God Shiva or those with Shivling. Within the temple, engage in puja ceremonies, offering prayers to God Shiva. Offer Abhishek (the ceremonial bathing of the Shiva Lingam) with sacred substances like water and milk. Due to time constraints and crowded temples, conducting full Abhishek rituals at home is advisable before visiting the temple. This allows for a more intimate and focused worship experience and partake in the collective energy of devotion.

Offer Abhishek at Temples to Shivling

1. Begin by ringing the bell to announce your presence and invoke the divine.

2. Offer water, milk and Bhel Patra(leaves) if allowed on the Shivling.

3. Clap three times to express devotion and awaken spiritual energy.

4. Perform half Parikarima (circumambulation) around the Shivling, starting clockwise from the front and circling until reaching the point where water flows out. Then, turn inwards, circling back to the starting point. Upon reaching the starting point, turn outward clockwise and exit, all while offering prayers.

5. Remember to say your heartfelt desire in Nandi's Ears.

6. Engage in meditation and chanting on Shiva, Om Namah Shivaya, fostering inner connection and spiritual growth.

Offer Puja at Home

Performing Puja at home offers a beautiful way to connect with the essence of God Shiva. Temples can be rushed, but taking time at home for this sacred ritual is a beautiful celebration of Maha Shivratri. Fasting is done from the evening before 6 p.m. on the day of Maha Shivratri to the next day. The fast is broken by going to Shiva Temple or home temple, taking prasad and blessings from the temple.

Prepare for the Puja

- Start this day by getting up early in Brahmmahurat before sunrise. The best time is between 3 am and 5.30 am.
- Clean and shower and set a serene atmosphere in your temple space.
- Carefully place the Shivling in a spacious container, ensuring the area is clean and suitable for spiritual practice.

Conduct the Sacred Shivling Puja

- Light fragrant incense to cleanse the air.
- Illuminate one diya, symbolizing enlightenment.
- Ring the bell/or Damru melodiously to summon divine presence.
- Tie a Moli to everyone involved, symbolizing divine protection.
- Illuminate the Shivling with a second diya and adorn it with a sacred thread, Moli.
- Tie the Janew to the Shivling and offer the second one. (if Janew available)
- Throughout the puja, immerse yourself in a meditative state, chanting "Om Namah Shivaya."

Perform the Abhishek of Shivling

- Gently pour water on top of the Shivling, invoking divine blessings.
- Offer and devotionally pour Panchamrit (follow the instructions on how to make it)
- Sugarcane Juice (if available)
- Mustard Oil (if available)
- Cleanse the Shivling once more with water.
- Adorn the Shivling with a divine (*Tripunda Tika*) with three lines of Ash, and then apply a sandalwood dot in the center.
- Apply Shiva's Tilak to everyone present in the Puja.

NOTE: Shiva's Tripunda Tika is applied by using the ring and middle fingers to draw two horizontal lines from left to right on the forehead. Then, the index finger is used to apply a third line below the first two. In the center of the lines, a sandalwood dot is applied with the middle finger.

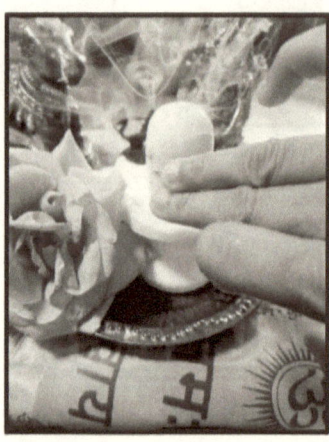

- Additionally, offer these to Shivling, *if available*:
- Offer a selection of five fruits. Try to include the "Ber" fruit (if available).
- Offer and grace the altar with seven White Flowers.
- Offer seven lotus buds (Kamal Gatte, if available).
- Offer your heartfelt desires woven into 108 grains of rice (filled with our aspirations done with the ritual a day before), presented lovingly to the divine.

Optional offerings rich in symbolism:

- Offer a single Clove, Black Pepper, and seven Sesame Seeds.

- Offer 1 Cardamom and 1 Clove.

- Offer 3 Paan and Supari.

- Offer 21 grains of Wheat.

- Offer and lay down seven Bhel Patr leaves, invoking sacredness and devotion.

- Offer and infuse the air with the ethereal fragrance of Ittar/perfume.

- Offer the sacred Dhatura if available.

- Offer Lentils – Red Masar, Yellow Arhar, and Green Moong.

- Offer the protective essence of 21 Peppercorns.

Conclude the puja

- Engage in a simple devotional or mala meditation with chant Om Namah Shivaya.
- Finish the puja with three resounding claps, awakening divine energy within and around.
- Spray a couple of drops of water under your seat and then gently touch this consecrated water to your forehead as a symbol of purification and divine connection.
- Complete your spiritual journey with a Half Parikarima around the Shivling, just like when we do Abhishek in the temple (explained earlier).

Capture the moments

As you capture traditions with photographs and videos, remember that you're not just celebrating a festival but keeping a rich cultural heritage alive. The pictures and videos will teach your children the steps of our traditions and the beauty of cherished memories.

The Great Night of Maha Shivratri

It is considered highly auspicious to stay awake throughout the night of Maha Shivratri. Many temples and religious places offer all-night performances and meditations, some of which are available online. Engage in a whole night of wakefulness and immerse yourself in the Great Night of Shiva. Take time to deeply reflect, seeking inner peace and spiritual growth. Let the Great Night guide your thoughts and prayers to deepen your connection with the divine. Let the Great Night of Devotion create a sense of peace akin to a tranquil melody.

The Next Day of Maha Shivratri

Maha Shivratri encapsulates a spiritual journey marked by devotion, prayer, and celebration. Finish your fast and the festival by going to the temple the next morning and taking Prasad as a blessing before you consume anything.

Clean the area and properly dispose of used offerings by placing them in the garden or plant soil facing north. Alternatively, you can immerse them in flowing water, such as a river or lake.

As the festivities conclude, they leave a sense of unity, peace, and divine connection that resonates deeply within our hearts and souls.

The Festival Legacy

Our festivals provide profound insights and enrich our understanding, underscoring the importance of honoring these traditions. Let the serenity of the festival linger in your heart, guiding your actions to live a divine life. May you become the guide who preserves and passes the sacred knowledge to our future generations.

Basant Panchami/Saraswati Jayanti

The Festival Calendar

Basant Panchami, celebrated in March in the English calendar and the month of Magh in the Indian calendar, marks the beginning of spring. It's named after "Basant," meaning spring, and "Panchami," the fifth day of Magh. This festival honors Saraswati, the Hindu Goddess of wisdom and arts, hence also called Sarasvati Jayanti.

The Festival Stories

A long time ago, when God Brahma, the creator, desired to bless the world with wisdom, he created Goddess Saraswati based on his kind thoughts. She was all about knowledge, music, art, and understanding. Saraswati is often depicted as clad in white, symbolizing purity, and playing the Veena, a string instrument, representing the harmony between knowledge and the arts. Her four arms symbolize the mind, brain, alertness, and knowing who you are. Basant Panchami/Saraswati Jayanti marks the arrival of Saraswati, the embodiment of wisdom, and the rejuvenating onset of spring. Adorned in bright yellow attire, individuals invoke Saraswati's blessings for enlightenment and personal advancement. It's a poignant moment for embarking on new journeys and aspiring towards academic and spiritual fulfillment.

The Festival celebration "step by step"

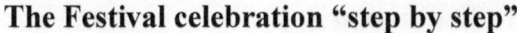

Basant Panchami is a time of vibrant colors, traditions, and fresh starts. Let's dive into the simplicity and joy of Basant, where the air is filled with the scent of flowers, the sky is decorated with colorful kites, and the atmosphere is alive with the spirit of new beginnings.

Prepare for the Festival

Ensure your home is clean and welcoming for the festivities. Prepare for the festival by freshening up, taking a shower, and dressing in traditional yellow attire. Yellow symbolizes the blooming of flowers, the renewal of nature, and the auspicious color associated with Saraswati.

Perform The Traditional Puja

Offer a traditional Puja and follow the steps of "How to Perform Puja," as outlined in the Puja chapter, taking the time to understand the meaning and purpose behind each ritual. If time is limited, follow the steps of "A Simple Daily Puja" with a simple prayer as described under "Puja and Prayer Methods." You can also simply chant the mantra for Saraswati, "Om Aim Saraswatyai Namah," and do a concluding blessing.

Commence Education Initiatives

- During the festival, teach children their first words to initiate them into language and communication, marking the commencement of their learning adventure.
- Enroll children in school to honor tradition and support their growth and development. Doing so sets them on a path toward a bright and successful future.

Celebrate with Community

Embrace the spirit of spring during the festival by participating in vibrant community activities. Join in the age-old tradition of kite flying, which holds significance in various parts of India. Gather with family and friends in open areas adorned with colorful kites, relishing the joy of flying them together. Alternatively, visit local temples and community centers to create and fly kites, fostering a sense of unity and celebration within the community.

Capture the Festival's Beauty

Be sure to capture the festival's beauty by taking pictures to celebrate, enjoy, and remember the moments together.

The Festival Legacy

To summarize, this festival traditionally emphasizes the importance of education, arts, and knowledge. It underscores the responsibility we have to pass down wisdom and education to our children, shaping their understanding and guiding their future. In this way, we honor Saraswati and ensure that our cultural legacy of learning and enlightenment thrives in the generations to come.

৩

Ram Navami

The Festival Calendar

Ram Navami typically falls in late March or early April, depending on the lunar calendar. This festival is celebrated on the ninth day of Chaitra month, according to the Hindu lunar calendar. This timing aligns with the end of Chaitra Navratri, a festival dedicated to Goddess Durga, and marks the birth anniversary of Lord Ram, the avatar of God Vishnu.

NOTE: If you are celebrating Chaitra Navratri, follow the guidelines on how to celebrate the festival as outlined for Navratri.

The Festival Stories

Ram Navami commemorates the birth of Lord Ram, a central figure in the Hindu epic, the Ramayana. According to the legend, King Dasharatha of Ayodhya, who had no heirs, performed a great sacrifice to be blessed with children. As a result, his queens bore him four sons, among whom was Lord Ram, born to Queen Kausalya. Rama's birth was foretold to bring peace and righteousness to the world, and his life is celebrated for embodying the virtues of truth, duty, and devotion.

The festival also symbolizes the triumph of good over evil. Lord Ram's life, marked by his devotion to dharma (righteousness), his exile, his battle against the demon king Ravan, and the rescue of his wife, Sita, serves as an ideal example of how to live a righteous and virtuous life. Ram Navami thus stands as a celebration of these ideals and a reminder of their importance in the spiritual and moral life of the devotee.

The Festival Celebration "Step by Step"

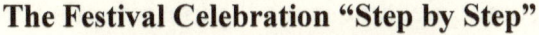

Ram Navami is a vibrant celebration of Lord Ram's birth, embodying the virtues of righteousness and devotion. Follow these steps to honor Lord Ram with heartfelt reverence and joy.

- Create a small altar with images or idols of Lord Ram, Sita, Lakshmana, and Hanuman. Decorate the altar with fresh flowers.

- Offer a traditional Puja and follow the steps of "How to Perform Puja," as outlined in the Puja chapter, taking the time to understand the meaning and purpose behind each ritual. If time is limited, follow the steps of "A Simple Daily Puja" with a simple prayer as described under "Puja and Prayer Methods."

- Visit Lord Ram's temple and listen to a recital of the Ramayana's significant episodes or engage in devotional prayers for him.

- Spend some quiet time in meditation, reflecting on the teachings and virtues of Lord Ram.

- Capture the magic through your camera, preserving moments that will teach children the value of tradition.

Celebrating Ram Navami is a profound tribute to Lord Ram's life and teachings. It infuses our lives with the values of righteousness, devotion, and integrity. It encourages us to walk the path of Dharma with the same grace and integrity that he exemplified throughout his journey.

The Festival Legacy

May this celebration inspire you and future generations to wholeheartedly embrace and follow the path of Dharma. May the lessons learned and the joy experienced guide and uplift future generations, enriching their lives with moral clarity and spiritual fulfillment.

Hanuman Jayanti

The Festival Calendar

Hanuman Jayanti is celebrated in late March or early April. It is observed on the 15th day of the Chaitra month in the Hindu lunisolar calendar, which usually corresponds to late March or early April. The celebration marks the birth anniversary of Lord Hanuman, a revered deity known for his strength, devotion, and courage.

The Festival Stories

Hanuman Jayanti commemorates the birth of Lord Hanuman, the devoted monkey Lord and a central character in the epic Ramayana. According to legend, Hanuman was born to Anjana and Kesari, who were blessed by God Shiva. His birth was a divine gift to aid Lord Ram in his battle against the demon king Ravan.

One of the most popular stories associated with Hanuman Jayanti is that of Hanuman's devotion to Lord Ram. When Sita was abducted by Ravan, Hanuman played a crucial role in locating her and delivering Rama's message. His strength, loyalty, and unwavering devotion helped in the successful rescue of Sita and the victory over Ravan.

Hanuman is celebrated for his boundless energy and commitment to righteousness. His life serves as an embodiment of selfless service, devotion, and strength, inspiring devotees to lead lives of integrity and faith.

The Festival Celebration "Step by Step"

Follow this step-by-step guide to celebrate Hanuman Jayanti, honoring Lord Hanuman with both devotion and simplicity. Craft a meaningful celebration that reflects his divine qualities and enriches your spiritual practice.

- Set up a special altar with images or idols of Lord Hanuman, along with pictures of Lord Ram, Lakshmana, and Sita. Adorn the altar with fresh flowers, a diya (oil lamp), and incense sticks to create a reverent space.
- Ensure to offer a puja dedicated to Lord Ram first before you offer the puja to Lord Hanuman.
- Follow the steps from the Puja Chapter to perform the traditional puja, taking the time to understand the meaning and purpose behind each ritual. If time is limited, follow the steps of "A Simple Daily Puja" with a simple prayer as described under "Puja and Prayer Methods." Offer sweets, such as laddoos and bananas, beloved by Lord Hanuman.

- Recite or listen to the Hanuman Chalisa to honor his divine presence.
- Spend some quiet time in meditation, reflecting on his teachings and how they can inspire and guide your daily life.
- Preserve the cherished moments and memories of the celebration with pictures and videos.

Celebrating Hanuman Jayanti is a profound tribute to Lord Hanuman's life and teachings, offering us a unique opportunity to reflect on and embrace his divine qualities. By honoring his unparalleled strength, unwavering devotion, and steadfast righteousness, we invite these virtues into our own lives, allowing them to enrich, guide, and inspire us in our daily journey.

The Festival Legacy

Hanuman Jayanti inspires us to embrace the divine virtues of devotion and service, as exemplified by Lord Hanuman. By honoring his teachings, you enrich the lives of those around you, instilling in them the spirit of unwavering devotion and selfless service.

Baisakhi

The Festival Calendar

"Baisakhi" is a term derived from the month of Vaisakh in the Indian calendar. It is celebrated on the 13th or 14th of April each year and coincides with the celebratory harvest season. The exact date on the English calendar may vary slightly from year to year due to its alignment with the lunisolar calendar used in India.

The Festival Stories

In India, Baisakhi is a special time when farmers celebrate the ripening of their crops after months of hard work. It's a joyful moment for them as they gather the fruits of their labor. But Baisakhi is more than just about the harvest; it's a reminder of how hard work leads to success, prosperity, and abundance. It underscores the importance of diligence, patience, and duty in achieving one's goals, serving as a poignant reminder of the connection between effort and reward.

The Festival Celebration "Step by Step"

As the auspicious day of Baisakhi unfolds, immerse yourself in rituals that honor the essence of renewal, abundance, and gratitude.

- Start your day with a devotional cleansing shower, envisioning the water as sacred, purifying, and blessing you. This ritual symbolizes the traditional sacred bath taken in India's holy rivers like the Ganges, marking the beginning of a day filled with spiritual reverence and gratitude.
- Perform puja and follow the steps of "How to Perform Puja," as outlined in the Puja chapter. If time is limited, follow the steps of "A Simple Daily Puja" as described under "Puja and Prayer Methods." Offer prayers to deities invoking their blessings.
- Join your community to celebrate the bountiful harvest through lively celebrations and performances at Baisakhi fairs.
- Take pictures to preserve the cherished moments and memories of the celebration.

The Festival Legacy

Baisakhi is a celebration of the fruits of hard work. It represents a time of gratitude for the labor that sustains us. Instilling these values in our children helps them appreciate the importance of dedication, perseverance, and the rewards of diligent effort, ensuring that the legacy of Baisakhi continues to inspire and guide them.

Teej or Teeya

The Festival Calendar

Teej, also known as Teeya, is a Punjabi Hindu festival that signifies the onset of the monsoon season and celebrates the union of God Shiva and Goddess Parvati. Teej usually happens in July or August in the English calendar. In the Hindu calendar, it's during the month of Sawan/Shravan. The dates may change each year based on the moon's cycle.

The Festival Stories

While the monsoon rains take center stage, Teej offers much more than a weather-related celebration. It's a day dedicated to the strength and spirit of women, embodied by the powerful Goddess Parvati, the wife of God Shiva. According to tradition, Parvati herself declared Teej a sacred day, promising blessings to those who seek her favor. This association with Parvati elevates Teej beyond a seasonal festival, transforming it into a celebration of Shakti, the divine feminine energy.

Women participate in the festivities by worshiping Parvati, seeing themselves as a reflection of the revered goddess. This beautiful tradition emphasizes the strength and essence within every woman, making the celebration meaningful and full of joy.

Teej coincides with the start of the rainy season in Punjab, which is crucial for the health of the soil and the successful growth of crops. The festival serves as a way of expressing gratitude for the rain and acknowledging its role in making the land fertile. It's a joyful celebration, expressing appreciation for the abundance and prosperity that the rain brings to our fields.

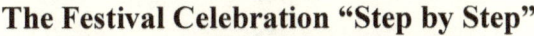

The Festival Celebration "Step by Step"

Embedded in love, this happy festival brings women together in dances, songs, and heartfelt devotions. Let's explore simple yet meaningful ways to enjoy the festival.

Prepare for the Festival

Married Women will adorn themselves in traditional attires and 16 solah shingar (16 items of adornment) listed below.

1. Mangtikka: Ornamental piece worn on the forehead.

2. Bindi: Decorative dot worn on the forehead.

3. Sindoor: Vermilion powder applied to the hair parting.

4. Kajal: Eyeliner applied to enhance the eyes.

5. Nath: A form of nose ring or pin worn on the nose.

6. Earrings: Ornamental earrings worn on the ears.

7. Mangalsutra or Necklace: Decorative chain worn around the neck.

8. Mehndi (Henna): Intricate designs applied on hands and feet.

9. Bangles: Ornamental bracelets worn on the wrists.

10. Gajra/Hairstyle: Elaborate hairstyle adorned with flowers or accessories.

11. Bajuband: Armlet worn on the upper arm.

12. Ring (Aarsi): Ring with a mirror attached.

13. Kamarband: Waistband worn around the waist.

14. Payal: Anklets worn around the ankles.

15. Bichua/Bichhiya: worn on the second toe.

16. Red Clothes: Red color clothes such as Lehanga or Chunni.

NOTE: Adorning oneself with Solah Shringar is not only a ritual but also a celebration of tradition, femininity, and auspiciousness, embodying the essence of Hindu customs and beliefs.

Perform Goddess Parvati Puja

Perform Parvati Puja during Teej to seek the blessings of Goddess Parvati. Please refer to the puja chapter for details on how to do the traditional puja, taking the time to understand the meaning and purpose behind each ritual. If time is limited, follow the steps of "A Simple Daily Puja" with a simple prayer as described under "Puja and Prayer Methods." Ensure to Invoke Goddess Parvati with an intention and Offer Kheer, Malpure, and Suji Halwa as bhog.

Swing with Ceremony

Dress up in vibrant traditional clothes, go to parks, and swing on decorated swings. The swings symbolize the playful and romantic relationship between God Shiva and Goddess Parvati. The swings mimic the gentle rain sway, celebrating the joy of the monsoon season.

Celebrate at Local Community/Temples

During this time, have fun at local fairs held in local community gatherings/ temples; happily, dance in colorful traditional clothes and sing sweet songs, adding beauty and joy to the celebration.

Capture the moments

Take a visual journey through the lens, encapsulating the beauty of the joy found in celebrating the festivals together.

As the festival concludes, its sweet notes linger, ensuring our cultural heritage lives on in the hearts of those who celebrate.

The Festival Legacy

Preserving our heritage is like holding onto the stories Grandma used to share—the tales that make our family history rich and vibrant. When we pass down these narratives and traditions to the younger ones, it's akin to gifting them a treasure chest filled with precious memories.

Rakhi- Raksha Bandhan

The Festival Calendar

Raksha Bandhan, also known as Rakhi, is a significant festival that revolves around the deep and cherished bond between brothers and sisters.

The name itself holds immense meaning – "Raksha" translates to "protection," and "Bandhan" signifies "bond" or "binding." Falling on the full moon day of the Shravan month in the Hindu calendar, typically July/August, Raksha Bandhan transcends biological ties, extending the sentiment of love and protection to cousins, friends, and even distant relatives.

The Festival Stories

Rakhi, the wonderful festival celebrating a special bond between brothers and sisters, has some exciting stories about how it all began. This day is about tying beautiful threads, called "rakhis," as a symbol of love and an unbreakable connection.

One of the most widely known narratives hails from the epic Mahabharata. In ancient India, Draupadi, the wife of the five Pandava brothers, was renowned for her intelligence, resilience, and noble character.

One day, in a moment of kindness, Draupadi noticed Lord Krishna had a small cut on his finger. Without hesitation, she tore a piece of her saree and gently tied it around Krishna's injured finger. Touched

242

by her compassionate act, Krishna pledged lifelong protection to Draupadi. This tale of Draupadi's generosity is woven into the celebration of Rakhi, symbolizing the enduring bond between siblings.

卍

Another tale states that in ancient India, there was a queen named Karnavati. She was concerned about her kingdom's safety, so she asked Emperor Humayun for help. As a symbol of her trust and a plea for protection, she sent him a special thread called Rakhi to the emperor. Touched by this gesture and recognizing the sacred bond symbolized by the thread, Emperor Humayun hurried to help her. This story teaches us that Rakhi is more than just a thread; it symbolizes love and protection, just like the strong bond between Queen Karnavati and Emperor Humayun.

These stories highlight the special relationship between brothers and sisters. Over time, people began celebrating this bond on a particular day called Rakhi/Raksha Bandhan.

The Festival Celebration "Step by Step"

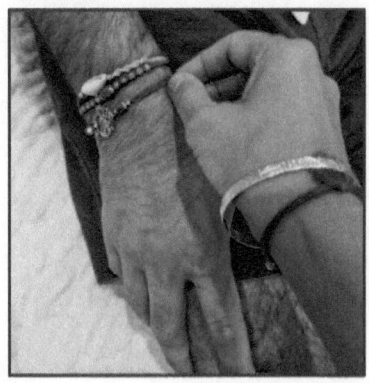

In the heartwarming celebration of Rakhi, a special bond between brothers and sisters takes center stage. As we explore the simple and meaningful ways to celebrate Rakhi, we honor the unique and cherished relationships that make this tradition so special.

Rakhi Check List

1. Rakhi

2. Puja Thali

3. Tilak

4. Unbroken Rice grains

5. Sweets for Brother

6. Gift/Money for Sister

Prepare for the Festival

Sisters Shopping: The festivities begin with sisters embarking on a joyful shopping spree. They meticulously choose Rakhis – intricately designed threads often adorned with beads, sequins, and colorful embellishments. Avoid Rakhis featuring God's depictions to maintain their sanctity. Sisters add a sweet touch to the celebration by also purchasing delectable sweets for their brothers.

Brothers Shopping: Not to be outdone, brothers eagerly reciprocate the love. They thoughtfully select gifts or money to present to their beloved sisters.

Perform the Ceremonial Puja

Perform the puja by following the steps outlined in the puja chapter.

- Commence the ceremony by ensuring you have all the necessary items for the puja.
- Perform Puja and follow the steps of "How to Perform Puja," as outlined in the Puja chapter, taking the time to understand the meaning and purpose behind each ritual. If time is limited, follow the steps of "A Simple Daily Puja" as described under "Puja and Prayer Methods." Now, offer sincere prayers to Lord Krishna, seeking blessings for the brother and sister.
- Ensure the brother is facing east for the ritual, and then proceed with gently applying a paste of vermilion and uncooked rice grains onto the brother's forehead using your ring finger, known as the tilak, symbolizing the auspicious occasion.

- Feed sweets to your brother, expressing your deep affection and warmest wishes.

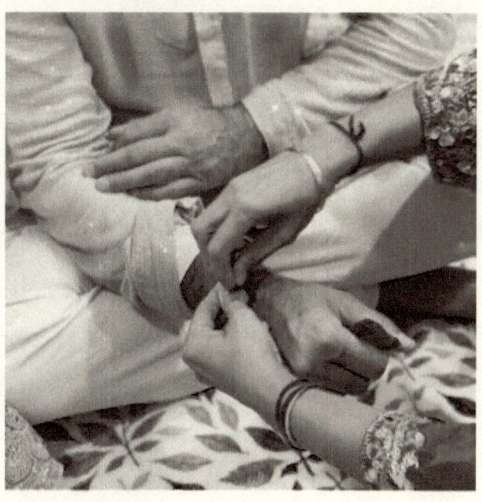

Perform the Sister's Rakhi Ritual and Offer Blessings

- At the heart of the ceremony, you will tie the Rakhi to your brother's right wrist. This sacred thread symbolizes the strong bond of love and your unwavering faith in his ability to protect you.
- After this, you will express your love and blessings to him.

Perform the Brother's Ritual and Offer Blessings

- After you tie the Rakhi, your brother will present his pre-chosen gifts or money to you. This act symbolizes his commitment to fulfilling your trust and offering you support and protection whenever needed.

- Following this, your brother will express his love and blessings to you.

Celebrate and Capture Memories

This post-ceremony gathering is a time for delicious food and the warmth of togetherness, making the celebration even more memorable. Capture these precious moments by taking pictures, preserving the joy of Raksha Bandhan for years to come.

NOTE: In today's world, Raksha Bandhan includes not just biological siblings but also distant ones, such as cousins and friends, underlining the values of respect and care. When distance keeps siblings apart, technology steps in. Sisters send Rakhis through the mail, and virtual ceremonies over video calls help maintain this cherished tradition, transcending geographical barriers.

The Festival Legacy

Passing on traditions like Rakhi is essential because they carry stories of love and family bonds. We keep our family's stories alive when we share these customs with younger ones. Sharing the stories and actively participating in the rituals allows younger siblings to understand the importance of family and the enduring love that binds them to their siblings.

Janam Ashtami

The Festival Calendar

Janmashtami is a Hindu festival that celebrates the birth of Lord Krishna, the eighth avatar (incarnation) of the revered deity God Vishnu. Usually falling in August or September in the English calendar, Janmashtami holds great importance in Hindu traditions.

"Janma" in Sanskrit means birth, and "Ashtami" refers to the eighth day in the Hindu lunar calendar. This festival is observed on the eighth day (Ashtami) of the Krishna Paksha (dark fortnight) in the month of Bhadrapada.

The Festival Stories

The legend behind Janmashtami unfolds in a time shrouded in darkness. Krishna was born to Devki and Vasudev, whom his maternal uncle, Kansa, imprisoned. Kansa was a cruel king, and his kingdom suffered because of his actions. A divine echo had told him that he would be killed by Devki and Vasudev's 8th child. Consumed by fear, Kansa imprisoned them and closely watched over them. With each child Devki bore, Kansa mercilessly took its life, determined to thwart the prophecy.

However, when Devki conceived her eighth child, a divine intervention occurred. Through his heavenly voice, the unborn Krishna assured his parents of his safety. Miraculously, on the night of his birth, the prison guards fell into a deep sleep, and the prison doors swung open. Vasudev, guided by divine instructions, carried the newborn Krishna across the raging Yamuna River to the village of Gokul, entrusting him to the care of his friend Nanda and his wife Yashoda.

Then Vasudev, in exchange, carried a baby girl born to his friend Nand on the same night and took the girl back to the prison. Meanwhile, back in the prison, Kansa, alerted by the birth cry, rushed in to find a baby girl. Blinded by rage, he runs to the prison and lifts the female child from her foot. When he is about to dash her against the wall, she slips from his grip, assuming the form of divine mother in the sky, revealing her true form as the divine protector Yogmaya and declaring that the destroyer of evil is flourishing in the Gokul.

In Gokul, people rejoiced at the birth of a son to Nand and Yashoda. Krishna's childhood in Gokul was filled with playful pranks and endearing miracles. He stole butter from gopis (milkmaids), charmed everyone with his mischievous smile, and vanquished ferocious demons like Putana. As he grew, he emerged as a fearless warrior, ultimately fulfilling the prophecy by slaying the tyrannical Kansa and restoring peace to the kingdom.

The Festival Celebration "Step by Step"

The celebration of Janmashtami is an occasion for devotees to remember and honor Lord Krishna's life, teachings, and divine presence. His birth is believed to signify the victory of good over evil and the establishment of dharma.

Prepare and Decorate

Spruce up your home with vibrant decorations and dress in themed attire, blending Western comfort with the festive spirit.

Conduct Puja

Offer a Puja to Lord Krishna and follow the steps of "How to Perform Puja," as outlined in the Puja chapter, taking the time to understand the meaning and purpose behind each ritual. If time is limited, follow the steps of "A Simple Daily Puja" with a simple prayer as described under "Puja and Prayer Methods."

Celebrate with the Community

Visit and enjoy local temples, community events, and performances that showcase various incidents from Krishna's life.

Participate in Handi Breaking

A significant highlight of Janmashtami is the 'Dahi Handi' ceremony, where teams of young men form human pyramids to reach and break a clay pot filled with curd, butter, and other treats suspended at a considerable height. This tradition symbolizes young Krishna's mischievous and playful nature, known for stealing butter from pots hung at a height.

Make Memories

Gather your friends and family members and enjoy the Handi Breaking at home or witness at temples. Find a small pot to represent the handi. Fill the pot with Yogurt, sweets, or small fruits inside. Choose an open area in your backyard or a spacious room. Suspend the handi at a manageable height. Then, gather around and take turns breaking the pot, using either your hands or a thin stick. Celebrate the moment with cheers and music and sharing the sweets from the broken pot. Remember to capture the joyous occasion by taking photos or videos to cherish the memories.

Safety is paramount, so ensure everyone participates in a safe environment. If children are joining, opt for a lower pot or a pinata, and make sure adults are there to supervise. If outdoor space is limited, consider doing it on a table indoors.

Janmashtami leaves, but the memories of Krishna's playfulness and teachings linger, making it a cherished part of our culture.

The Festival Legacy

Continuing ancestral traditions, especially during festivals like Janmashtami, helps us keep family stories alive. When we celebrate, we're not just following rituals; we're sharing stories our grandparents shared with us. It's like passing on a treasure chest of memories from one generation to the next. May the spirit of Janmashtami fill your life with joy, devotion, and a renewed sense of cultural connection!

ॐ

Ganesh/Ganesha Chaturthi

The Festival Calendar

Ganesh Chaturthi is a significant Hindu festival celebrated to honor the birth of Lord Ganesh, the son of God Shiva and Goddess Parvati. This festival typically takes place in September, the Hindu month of Bhadrapada. It spans ten days and concludes with the immersion of Ganesh idols in water known as Visarjan.

The Festival Stories

The legend behind Ganesh Chaturthi is as heartwarming as it is profound. Nestled amidst the snow-capped peaks of Kailash Mountain, there lived God Shiva and Goddess Parvati. People loved this heavenly couple. One day, Shiva was away helping others. Parvati desired to take a bath and wanted to have someone to guard and protect her privacy. Parvati, using the finest clay, meticulously crafted a cute little boy with her hands and named him her son, Ganesh. She infused life into the clay, giving Ganesh the task of guarding and protecting the entrance, with strict instructions not to allow anyone to enter.

As fate would have it, when Parvati was taking a bath, Shiva came home. Ganesh stopped him from entering Parvati's room. Ganesh, wanting to protect his mom's privacy, bravely stood his ground. This led to a confrontation between Shiva and Ganesh, culminating in a tragic turn of events. In a moment of misunderstanding, Shiva severed Ganesh's head.

When Parvati came back, she found Ganesh lifeless and felt very sad. Her grief was immeasurable. She begged Shiva to bring their son back. Touched by Parvati's love, Shiva promised to give Ganesh a new head and embarked on a quest to find a solution.

Shiva's Ganas (celestial helpers) searched the entire universe for a new head for Lord Ganesh; they returned with the head of a mighty elephant named Airavata. Airavata belonged to Indra, the king of gods, and his willingness to sacrifice his own head for Ganesh's restoration signifies supreme devotion and loyalty to the divine. This noble act restored Ganesh to life and symbolized the interconnectedness of all beings in the cosmic order. It emphasizes themes of selflessness, sacrifice, and the boundless compassion of the divine.

After this event, Shiva declared Ganesh as the primary deity to be worshipped first in any ritual to seek blessings for a smooth and obstacle-free experience. This story underscores the values of humility, devotion, and overcoming challenges, establishing Ganesh as a cherished deity in Hinduism.

The Festival Celebration "Step by Step"

The ten days of Ganesh Chaturthi are a sacred journey of welcoming Lord Ganesha into our homes and hearts, seeking his blessings for wisdom, prosperity, and the removal of obstacles, and lovingly bidding him farewell on the tenth day. These days symbolize life's profound cycles—birth, growth, and release—teaching us to cherish new beginnings, embrace growth, and gracefully let go. They bring families and communities together in devotion and joy, creating a deeper connection to the divine and reminding us of the infinite presence of Lord Ganesha in our lives.

Get a Ganesh Idol

Make/craft/buy a small clay, brass, copper, or silver statue of Lord Ganesh.

Prepare the Altar

Clean the home before the festival and prepare the altar for Ganesh. Place the idol of Ganesh for the festival on this altar. Make the puja area pretty with colorful decorations.

Daily Puja Sadhana

If time permits, dedicate ten days to offering a traditional puja, following the sacred steps outlined in the Puja chapter. For those with limited time, embrace a simplified daily puja sadhana for ten days, allowing you to connect with divine energies while honoring the essence of the ritual. Offer Ganesha's favorite sweets, such as modaks, if available. You can also chant "Om Gam Ganapataye Namah" 108 times with a mala.

Symbolic Visarajan

After ten days of celebrating with Ganesh, it's time for a symbolic farewell. For clay idols, immersion in a body of water signifies the return to nature, reminding us of the impermanence of all things. Grand Visarjan (immersion) ceremonies in India occur in various regions, where idols are immersed in lakes and oceans.

Statues made of copper, brass, or silver can be given a ceremonial bath and placed back in the temple.

Cherish the Moments

As you capture cherished memories with photographs, remember that you're not just celebrating a festival but keeping a rich cultural heritage alive. Encourage everyone's participation and foster the continuation of this cherished tradition.

The Festival Legacy

As we finish celebrating Ganesh Chaturthi, remember the joy we had. Doing these rituals at home is not just about tradition; it's about keeping these practices alive and feeling connected to our heritage. Let's make these celebrations part of our family story, passing on our traditions to the next generation.

Navratri/Narate/Durga Asthami

Narate/Durga Ashtami/Navratri marks a special Nine day of celebration and fasting dedicated to honoring nine different forms of Goddess Durga.

Day 1: Shailaputri - This day celebrates Durga as the daughter of the mountains, symbolizing unshakeable strength and grounding.

Day 2: Brahmacharini - Here, Durga is worshipped for knowledge, perseverance, and self-discipline.

Day 3: Chandraghanta - Meaning "moon-bellied," this day honors Durga's beauty and serenity, reminding us of the calming influence of inner peace.

Day 4: Kushmanda - This day is dedicated to Durga's radiant form, illuminating the world and dispelling darkness.

Day 5: Skandamata - As Skandamata, Durga is depicted as a loving mother, highlighting the nurturing and protective aspects of the divine feminine.

Day 6: Katyayani - This day honors Durga's fierce warrior spirit and unwavering courage in adversity.

Day 7: Kalratri - Meaning "dark night," this day is dedicated to Durga's powerful form that destroys negativity and ignorance.

Day 8: Mahagauri - Here, Durga is worshipped in her serene white form, symbolizing purity, peace, and forgiveness.

Day 9: Siddhidatri - The ninth day, also known as Durga Navami, celebrates Durga's ultimate form, the embodiment of perfection and the granter of wishes

NOTE: Many people complete their fast on Ashtami, the eighth day of Navratri, which honors Goddess Durga's victory over demons such as Chand, Mund, Rakthabij, and Mahishasur. Others extend their observance to the ninth day.

Day 10, Vijayadashami or Dussehra, follows Navratri and celebrates Goddess Durga's triumph over all demons. It also marks Lord Ram's victory over Ravan, aided by Goddess Durga, emphasizing the theme of Durga's conquest and triumph over evil. This day is observed as Dussehra, a festival that will be explained in detail later.

The Festival Calendar

Navratri is observed several times a year, each with its unique significance. Below are the details of these occasions.

Paush Ashtami/Navratri: This festival occurs during the Hindu month of Paush (December-January). Legend says that the goddess was incarnated as Shakambhari during this time to alleviate famine and food crises on Earth. Paush Navratri involves various rituals, prayers, and fasting to seek blessings from the divine feminine.

Gupt/Magha Navratri: Magh Navratri, also known as Gupt Navratri or Magha Navaratri, is a Hindu festival dedicated to Goddess Durga, typically occurring in Magha (January-February) over nine days. Beyond public celebration, it holds significance in esoteric and tantric circles. For tantriks and spiritual seekers, it takes on a deeper, more mystical dimension, with specialized rituals aimed at harnessing divine feminine energies, often in secrecy. People engage in chanting prayers, performing puja, and fasting to seek blessings from Goddess Durga, fostering spiritual growth, inner strength, and protection from negative energies. Fasting symbolizes self-control and dedication to the divine, inviting Durga's presence as a shield against adversities and malevolent forces.

Chaitra Navratri: Celebrated in March or April, Chaitra Navratri marks the beginning of the Hindu New Year. During this Navratri, devotees worship Goddess Durga to invoke her blessings for prosperity, success, and happiness in the new year. The festival culminates with Ram Navami, the birthday of Lord Ram, which falls on the ninth day of Navratri. Devotees celebrate Ram Navami with prayers and bhajans (devotional songs) honoring Lord Ram's life and teachings and visit temples to offer their prayers.

Sharad Navratri: This widely celebrated festival falls in September or October and signifies the onset of the autumn season. It commemorates the victory of good over evil and the triumph of Lord Ram over the demon king Ravan. Devotees fast and pray for nine days, seeking the blessings of Goddess Durga to overcome obstacles and attain spiritual upliftment. The festival culminates with Dussehra on the 10th day, which marks Lord Ram's victory and Ravan's defeat, symbolizing the triumph of righteousness over evil.

During Sharad Navratri, in many regions of India, devotees worship Sanjhi Mata, who is considered a manifestation of Goddess Durga, with great fervor and devotion. To honor her, people create cow dung artworks depicting scenes from her life. During the nine-day festival, prayers, songs, and rituals are performed, with offerings of vegetarian food made daily. Planting barley/Jao/wheatgrass seeds in front of the Goddess symbolizes blessings for health and wealth. The festival concludes with the artworks being immersed in water during Dussehra Day.

In many regions of India, during Sharad Navratri, people also participate in the Ahoi Ashtami Ritual, which is held in many regions of India. Mothers make or buy an Ahoi Ashtami calendar. They place it alongside a sacred 'Kalash' copper/silver water pot filled with water, adorned with a Swastik and a holy thread, next to an image of Ahoi Mata calendar. Mothers lovingly write their (sons) children's names on the calendar during Navratri, preparing for the Ahoi Ashtami Fast and Puja. For information on the Ahoi Fast, which usually takes place about eight days before Diwali and four days after Karwa Chauth (dates may vary each year), please refer to the chapter on observing traditional fasts.

Ashad Navratri: Additionally, some regions may observe Ashad Navratri, which falls in the Hindu month of Ashadha, usually in June or July. However, Ashad Navratri is not as widely celebrated as the four types mentioned above.

Each type of Navratri has its unique cultural and spiritual significance, emphasizing the importance of seeking divine blessings, celebrating the victory of good over evil, and fostering spiritual growth and harmony.

The Festival Stories

During Navratri, nine primary forms of the Goddess are revered, each symbolizing the triumph over demons and the eradication of evil. Every day of the festival is dedicated to a specific form of the goddess, commemorating her victories against various malevolent forces and demons.

The main story is about a powerful and mean demon king named Mahishasur. Because he was very cruel, he became a big problem for humans and gods. He offered prayers and meditations to please God Brahma and get even more power. As a reward, Brahma gave him an extraordinary power that made him almost unbeatable. This power said that no Man or God could defeat him.

With this extraordinary power, Mahishasura took control of heaven, kicking out the gods and scaring everyone. The gods in heaven got worried and had to ask God Shiva for help. In response, Shiva and other gods joined their powers and asked for help from Goddess Durga (Parvati's Avatar), a mighty warrior with divine energy called Shakti. Mounted on a powerful lion, Durga, with her ten arms wielding an array of weapons, embarked on a fierce battle against the demon Mahishasur.

For nine gruelling days and nights, the earth trembled with the clash of their powers. Mahishasur, drawing upon his demonic might, displayed an arsenal of fearsome attacks. But Durga, unwavering in her resolve and fueled by her divine purpose, countered every blow. Finally, on the tenth day, called Vijayadashami or Dussehra, Goddess Durga delivered the final decisive strike, vanquishing the demon king and restoring peace to the heavens and earth.

The epic battle between Durga and Mahishasur signifies the eternal struggle between good and evil, light and darkness. Durga's triumph is a powerful reminder that even in the face of immense adversity, with unwavering courage and righteous action, victory is possible.

The Festival Celebration "Step by Step"

Here, you will find two approaches to festival celebrations: a simple version and a detailed one. Whether you're just starting or have been celebrating for years, the essence of these festivals lies in the devotion with which they are observed. Both methods honor the divine spirit, emphasizing that any celebration, when approached with sincere reverence, is truly meaningful and cherished.

Simple Steps for a Meaningful Celebration

These instructions, simple yet powerful, will enrich your festival experience, ensuring each moment is memorable and fulfilling.

Prepare for the Festival

Clean your home and temple thoroughly before the festival begins, and obtain a clay, brass, or copper statue or a printed image of Goddess Durga to worship at home or in the temple.

Perform Daily Puja for Nine Days

Perform a daily Puja by following the steps outlined in the Puja chapter. Offer a Puja and follow the steps of "How to Perform Puja," as outlined in the Puja chapter, taking the time to understand the meaning and purpose behind each ritual. If time is limited, follow the steps of "A Simple Daily Puja" with a simple prayer as described under "Puja and Prayer Methods."

Meditate or recite the "Om Dum Durgaya Namah" mantra 108 times and remember to pay a visit to the temple on one of the days of Navratri.

Fast for the Festival

Observe a fast throughout the nine days of Navratri. If unable to fast for the entire period, a one-day fast is also acceptable. Some people follow a vegetarian diet if fasting is not an option.

Perform Kanya Puja on the 8th/9th Day of the Festival

The fast concludes with Kanya Puja on Durga Navami, the ninth day of Navratri. However, in some regions, it concludes on Ashtami, the eighth day. This ritual holds immense significance as it involves worshipping young girls, who are seen as manifestations of divine feminine energy. For Kanya Puja, please see the process explained in detail below.

If hosting Kanya Puja is challenging, consider setting aside funds for the girls, along with sweets and money, and donating to a temple as an alternative expression of devotion.

Gratefulness Immersion on the 10th day

As an act of gratitude and closure, perform the Immersion ritual on the 10th day of Navratri if statues made of clay are purchased. Gently immerse the clay Goddess statue in a container filled with water or in a flowing river/stream/ ocean, symbolizing the conclusion of the festival and the culmination of prayers and devotion offered over the nine days. If using Brass/Silver/Copper Statue, devotionally bathe them and place them back in the temple.

Celebrate with the Community

Join the festive spirit by participating in Dandia Dance. Dress in traditional attire and engage in garba and dandia dances organized in temples and community centers. Dandiya dance is a traditional Indian folk dance associated with Navratri, celebrating the divine feminine energy, especially that of Goddess Durga. The circular dance symbolizes the cyclical nature of life, with its energetic beats reflecting the triumph of positive forces.

A detailed Celebration of the Navratri Festival with Rituals

Please note that any rituals outlined in this section can also be incorporated into simple celebrations. Based on your devotional preferences and desires, you may choose to offer one, multiple, or all offerings in simple or detailed celebration.

Navratri Shopping List

Select and prepare to offer one, multiple, or all offerings based on your devotional preferences and desires.

- Puja supplies (please see the puja chapter)
- Rangoli supplies
- clay/brass/copper statues or print-out images
- Brass/Copper/Clay Pitcher
- Unbroken Grains of Rice
- Ganga Jal

- Grass (Dhurva)
- Betel Nut/Supari (1)
- Mango Leaves or Betel Leaves (5)
- Coconut (1)
- fruits (for nine days offering)
- Cardamoms, Cloves and Misri (for 9 days offering)
- Unsweetened Makhane (for 9 days offering)
- One-dollar coins or any amount of money you can afford (for 9 days offering)
- Wheatgrass/Jau/Barley seeds and Soil (devotional)
- Hindu flag of Mata Durga (devotional)
- Toran made from 5/11/21, Mango Leaves or ready-made (devotional)
- 27 paan leaves for garland (devotional)
- Yellow and red flowers (devotional)
- Rose Ittar or perfume or Rose Water (devotional)
- Clay pots /Water Container (devotional)
- Fasting foods: Nuts and dried fruits, Rock salt (Sendha namak) and Fresh fruits (for fasts)
- Makeup and jewelry items,16 Shingar items (for temple offering)
- Gifts for Kanya/Kanjak Puja on Ashtami/Navami (devotional)

Prepare for the Festival

Thoroughly clean and decorate the house with Rangoli to welcome the festival's auspiciousness. Purchase the supplies needed for the nine days or purchase them as needed.

Commencement Rituals

Perform one, multiple, or all rituals based on your devotional preferences and desires.

- Hang a Hindu flag of Mata Durga on your roof for auspicious beginnings.
- Place a vessel filled with water at the main entrance door and add yellow and red flowers towards the north/east side.
- Make a Swastika with red kumkum (tika) at the entrance of the front door to invite good fortune and prosperity.
- Make or buy a toran (a traditional decoration hung on doorways to invite blessings) using 5, 11, or 21 mango leaves, and hang it in front of your home. A toran made with moli or red thread adds an auspicious touch.

Sacred Ghat/Kalsh/Pitcher Sthapana Ritual

This sacred ritual is profoundly symbolic and shall be done with respect and devotion. This Ritual symbolically represents our connection from earth to the Divine in the spiritual world.

- Clean the space where You will place the Sacred Pitcher/Kalsh.
- Gather a small clay, brass or copper pitcher and place it on a plate filled with unbroken grains of rice or Jau. This pitcher represents the womb of Mother Nature, signifying the source of all creation.
- Use red tilak powder to draw a swastika on the pitcher. This symbolizes auspicious beginnings.
- Tie moli (red thread) around the pitcher, circling it three or nine times. The red thread represents the Mahamaya, the cosmic force that is both the beginning and the end of everything.

- Fill the pitcher with clean water and Ganga Jal. This represents purity and spiritual cleansing.

- Offer a prayer to Lord Ganesha to remove all obstacles from your path, then recite "Om Dum Durgaya Namah" to invoke the blessings of Mother Durga while doing the ritual.

- Illuminate the space by lighting a lamp and burning incense to create a spiritual ambiance and connection.

- Add fresh flowers, unbroken rice, turmeric, tilak powder, Ganga Jal, grass (Dhurva), one Betel nut (supari), one cardamom pod, one clove, and a one-dollar coin as symbols of offerings to the Mother Goddess into the pitcher.

- Top it with five mango leaves or betel leaves, symbolizing five elements of this earthly world.

- Finally, position a coconut wrapped in Red Cloth on top of the leaves, ensuring that the "eye" of the coconut faces you. This coconut represents your physical body. This symbolic gesture represents the connection between the divine and the material world.

- During All Nine days of Puja, Offer a Prayer to the Sacred Pitcher.

- On Visarjan day, the final day of Navratri, you can place the coconut from the pitcher in the temple, offer it to flowing water in a river or lake, or consume it as prasad. Sprinkle water from the pitcher around the house and pour some into the plants. Gather all the ingredients from the pitcher, along with some Jau (barley/wheatgrass), and wrap them in a red cloth. Place this in a safe or in your business or workplace to invoke the goddess's blessings until the next Navratri. Any items can be respectfully buried in the earth or offered to the flowing water.

Navratri Khetri Ritual

The khetri grown during Navratri symbolizes the spiritual journey of the devotee. Just as the seeds of jau (barley) or wheatgrass sprout and grow into lush, green leaves, the devotee's inner potential blossoms through devotion and ritual. In the beginning, the seeds are buried beneath the soil, representing the latent spiritual energy within, waiting to be awakened. With care, nurturing, and the right conditions and guidance, the devotee cultivates the soul through consistent practice, devotion, and discipline.

The green leaves and shoots that emerge signify spiritual growth—the unfolding of inner wisdom and the blossoming of divine energy within. As the khetri reaches toward the sky, so too does the devotee ascend to higher states of consciousness, leaving behind the ignorance of the material world. This growth mirrors the journey from the soul's dormant state to the realization of divine oneness, making Navratri a powerful reminder of our own spiritual potential and transformation.

Select a Clay Pot: Choose a clean clay pot for the ritual.

Draw a Swastika: Carefully create a swastika symbol on the pot to invite blessings.

Tie Moli Thread: Wrap the moli (red thread) around the pot to enhance its auspiciousness.

Fill with Soil: Add fresh soil to the pot, filling it about halfway.

Sow the Seeds: Add jau (barley) seeds or wheatgrass seeds into the soil.

Recite a Prayer: Say a heartfelt prayer to the Goddess while sowing the seeds.

Water the Seeds: Gently water the seeds, using Ganga Jal if available, for added sanctity.

Nurture the Soil: Add more soil, then place a lid on the pot for a couple of days to create a nurturing environment. Let the seeds grow leaves for nine days. Ensure the soil remains slightly damp throughout the nine days to promote the growth of Khetri.

Note: During the specific Sharad Navratri ONLY, on the 10th day, which is the Dussehra festival, sisters place these leaves on brothers' ears or caps in a ritual that is explained in the Dusshera festival.

Fasting For the Festival

Prepare to fast, following your family traditions with dedication. If fasting for the entire period isn't feasible, consider fasting for one day or eating vegetarian meals.

NOTE

For Sharad Navratri ONLY, participate in the Ahoi Ashtami Ritual and Fast if it is part of your family tradition and you wish to continue the practice. Please check the Fasts chapter of the book for more details on Ahoi Fast. For the Ritual, Mothers make or buy an Ahoi Ashtami calendar. They place it alongside a sacred 'Kalash' copper/silver water pot filled with water, adorned with a Swastik and a holy thread, next to an image of Ahoi Mata. Then, Plant barley or wheatgrass in front of the altar for nine days. Mothers lovingly write their children's names on the calendar during Navratri, preparing for the Ahoi Ashtami Fast Puja that comes after Karwa Chauth. (Please check the dates, as they may change yearly.

For Sharad Navratri ONLY, participate in the Sanjhi Mata ritual if it is a part of your family tradition, and you wish to continue the practice. You can adapt the ritual by creating Sanjhi Mata artwork with materials like paper and clay and setting up a home altar with flowers and images of the goddess. Plant barley or wheatgrass in front of the altar for nine days. Throughout the nine-day festival, perform daily prayers and sing/play devotional songs or prayers. *The festivities culminate on Dussehra day with the immersion of these artworks in water, marking the end of the celebration.*

While replicating such vibrant traditions in the Western world can be challenging, devotion remains a universal thread connecting all cultures.

Meditation and Sadhana Routine

Puja of the Divine Goddess

Offer a Puja and follow the steps of "How to Perform Puja," as outlined in the Puja chapter, along with the following steps.

- Spray Rose Water daily in the home, starting in the north direction and then in all directions, and be grateful to the goddess in life.
- Chant "Om Dum Durgaya Namah" 108 times with Japa Mala to invoke divine blessings.
- Listen online or Read the Book Durga Saptashati (If read, to be finished through 9 days of the festival) to receive blessings from the goddess.
- Meditate on the form of the Devi of the day for a few minutes to connect with the divine energy.

Offerings to the Divine Goddess

You may choose to offer one, multiple, or all offerings based on your devotional preferences and desires.

- Offering fruits to the Goddess daily Represents offering the best of what we have to the divine. These fruits can be consumed after puja as Prasad is blessed by the divine.

- Offering 7 cardamoms and Misri to the goddess daily symbolizes purity, health, sweetness, and prosperity, and to seek her divine blessings.

- Offering 2 cloves daily represents protection and warding off negative energies.

- Offering a few unsweet Makhane and a one-dollar coin daily, signifying wealth and prosperity.

- Offering 16 Solah Shingar (Makeup and Jewellery items) on any day in the temple symbolizes adorning the deity with love and devotion, enhancing the spiritual connection with the divine.

- Offering a garland made of 27 Paan Leaves symbolizes receiving the desired boon from the goddess. As you make the garland, with each leaf, say your wish/desire to the goddess (a total of 27 times), tie it with Moli, and offer this garland to the Goddess in the temple during any nine days of this festival.

Durga Ashtami/Kanya/Kanjak/Lonkadiya Puja

The conclusion of fasting often coincides with Kanya Puja on Durga Navami, the ninth day of Navratri, although in some regions, it concludes on Asthami, the 8th day. Please see the detailed Puja ritual below.

Day 10 Finishing Rituals

- On the 10th day of Navratri, immerse the clay Goddess statue in a water-filled container, an ocean, or a flowing river, or bury it in the earth under a tree, bidding farewell to symbolize the festival's conclusion. If you have brass, silver, or copper statues, just give them a devotional bath and place them back in your temple.

- Place the barley leaves in a red cloth in a safe/locker and consume some as blessings.

- Donate Makhane and coins to the poor.

- Consume Cardamom and Misri as a blessing.

- Consume cloves or offer them at the temple.

Community Fun Festivities

Join the festive spirit by participating in Dandia Dance for Navratri, mostly done during Sharad Navratri. Dress in traditional attire and engage in garba and dandia dances organized in temples and community centers. Dandiya dance is a traditional Indian folk dance associated with Navratri, celebrating the divine feminine energy, especially that of Goddess Durga. The circular dance symbolizes the cyclical nature of life, with its energetic beats reflecting the triumph of positive forces.

Kanya Puja/Ashtami (8/9th day of the festival) Process

Girls are called Kanjkas or kanyas, and Boys are called Lonkadiyas.

This significant ritual involves worshipping young girls as manifestations of divine feminine energy. If hosting the puja is challenging, consider setting aside funds for the girls, accompanied by sweets, and donating to a temple as an alternative gesture of devotion.

Puja Check List

1. Flowers
2. Rice grains and Vermillion for Tilak
3. Prasad made of Puri, Kale Chane, and Halwa cooked
4. Moli thread
5. Jewellery such as hairbands, bindis etc.
6. Notebooks and pens

7. Fruit

8. Money

Puja Process

You can visit a temple to do a Puja ceremony there, or you can choose to host Kanjkas/girls and Lonkadiyas/Langurs/Boys at your home, following the traditional practice observed in India.

Invitation

Gather a group of 9 young girls and 2 boys, all under the age of 10, to join in the puja at your home or temple. These girls symbolize the 9 manifestations of Goddess Durga, while the boys represent the embodiments of Ganesh and Bhairv. It's believed that the presence of Ganesh and Bhairv is essential for completing any puja dedicated to the Goddess. If it's not feasible to gather the exact numbers, a minimum of 2 girls and one boy would suffice to uphold the significance of the ritual.

Purify and Decorate

Cleanse the space where the puja will take place. And on the ground, have a clean cloth for them to sit on.

Welcome Ritual

Greet the girls and boys with respect and affection. Wash the feet using water mixed with turmeric and flowers as a mark of reverence.

Holistic Ritual

Perform the ritualistic bath by sprinkling water on their heads and offering flowers while reciting mantras (Om Dum Durgayai Namah). Tie Moli to their wrists and do the Tilak ceremony (with the Right-Hand Ring finger) as a Puja ritual.

Adorn with Gifts

Gift them with bangles, sweets, fruits, study items, and other items as you desire. Traditionally, they're also given some money.

Offer Food and Fruits

Offer prasad (sacred food) consisting of puri, halwa, and chana (black chickpeas). If you are unable to cook, you can always give store-bought sweets.

Seek Blessings

As the girls and boys prepare to leave your home, bow respectfully and touch their feet, acknowledging them as manifestations of Goddess Durga, Lord Ganesh, and Bhairav. Seek their blessings by offering them rice grains and inviting them to place the grains in your hands or within the folds of your scarf (jholi). Ask them to adorn you with a tika and place their hands on your head to bless you. Later, store these blessed grains in a safe or secure place, cherishing them as sacred tokens of their blessings.

Cherish Memories

Capture precious memories by taking numerous pictures and videos, sharing the experience with your family, and sowing the seeds of curiosity and significance among them. Encourage everyone's participation and foster the continuation of this cherished tradition.

As the Navratri celebration bids goodbye, hearts are filled with the divine energy of Goddess Durga. Until next Navratri, the memories of these auspicious days will remain a cherished part of our spiritual journey.

The Festival Legacy

To pass on the legacy of Navratri, it is important to involve younger generations in the festival's celebrations. Sharing stories of Goddess Durga's victories and the significance of each ritual helps cultivate an appreciation for the festival's spiritual depth. Encouraging participation in traditional practices such as preparing special foods, participating in Garba dances, and attending temple services creates opportunities for experiential learning and strengthens familial and cultural bonds.

Karva Chauth

The Festival Calendar

Karva Chauth is a beautiful celebration of love and devotion in October/ November. "Karva" means pot (used in the ceremony), and "Chauth" means 4th. This festival falls on the 4th day of the dark fortnight, or Krishna Paksha, in the month of Kartik in the Hindu Calendar, holding immense significance in Hindu culture.

The Festival Celebration "Step by Step"

As the auspicious day of Karva Chauth dawns, a heartwarming atmosphere filled with love and commitment washes over married couples. During Karva Chauth, wives observe a strict fast throughout the day, expressing their deepest wishes for their husbands' long and healthy lives. This heartfelt gesture is reciprocated by the husbands, who shower their wives with gifts like clothing, jewelry, and other desired items.

Note: Unmarried girls can also participate in the fast, dedicating their prayers from sunrise to the appearance of the evening stars, anticipating a future blessed with love and a happy marriage.

Karwa Chauth Checklist

- Mother-in-law: prepares "Sargi" – a delightful assortment of sweets, savory snacks like matthi, fruits, nuts, and containers for Daughter-in-law.

- Daughter-in-law: organizes money, nuts, and sweets for Mother-in-law.

- Daughter-in-law's family: arranges sweets, gifts, and money for son-in-law's Family *(ONLY For the First Year of Marriage)*.

- Husband: purchases clothing, jewelry, or gifts for wife.

NOTE: This festival encompasses many rich rituals, each with its own significance. It is advisable to take notes, pictures, and videos to capture the details of these traditions as you celebrate the festival. This way, you can explain, preserve, and pass on these meaningful practices to your children, ensuring they remain a cherished part of your family's heritage.

Essential Supplies

- Small water pots, traditionally made of earth (stainless steel used nowadays)

- Karwa Chauth plate, including a pot, sieve, and a candle

- Henna, bangles, makeup, and other jewelry

- Feniya, a dessert made with boiled milk, sugar, and delicate noodles

- Mathi Sweet and Salty

- Sweets for the festival

- Goddess Durga or Parvati Statue or Idol or Picture

- Moli thread and Tilak (Vermillion) with unbroken rice grains

- Rice, lentils, and Vegetables for the feast

The Day Before Karva Chauth

- The mother-in-law/elder woman in the family prepares sargi, a thoughtful assortment of sweets and salty snacks like Mathi, fruits, nuts, and containers. This aids the daughter-in-law in preparing for the fast, as it's believed that consuming Sargi provides the strength needed for the day.

- The Daughter-in-law prepares a special gift, known as Baiya, for the mother-in-law or an elderly woman in the household. This thoughtful gesture includes money, nuts, and sweets.

- The husband takes center stage by purchasing beautiful clothing, jewelry, or thoughtful gifts for his wife, expressing his love and gratitude for her devotion.

- Women acquire small water pots, traditionally made of earth but often replaced with stainless steel nowadays, for the ceremony.

- In anticipation of the fasting day, women prepare a beautifully arranged Karwa Chauth plate, including a plate, pot, sieve, and candle.
- Women enhance their beauty by adorning themselves with henna and bangles, preparing for the fast day.
- *In the first year of marriage*, a tradition unfolds where everyone in the son-in-law's home receives sweets, gifts, and money to mark the joyous occasion from the bride's family.

The Morning of Karwa Chauth

As the first rays of dawn paint the sky, women rise with quiet determination. Around 5 am, it's time for the pre-dawn meal. This meal often consists of Feniya, a light and sweet noodle dish, or a simple vegetarian meal that provides sustenance before the fast begins. Some women enjoy a cup of comforting chai as well. Once the pre-dawn meal is complete, the women embark on the fast, cherishing the festival's significance, expressing love for their partner, and sending heartfelt wishes for their enduring happiness.

Additional activities

- Women embrace the festive spirit by adorning makeup and jewelry.
- For those who haven't done so already, applying intricate henna designs on their hands and arms enhances the festive spirit and adds a touch of elegance.

- Visiting a temple for a puja (prayer ceremony) allows women to connect with their faith and offer heartfelt prayers for their husbands' well-being.

Note: On this day, activities like cleaning, needlework, or washing hair are avoided.

The Afternoon of Karwa Chauth, Puja/Story Time

The focus shifts towards puja and storytelling in the afternoon (around 2/3 PM). A dedicated space is thoughtfully organized and arranged for the puja and storytelling session.

- Women meticulously prepare their Puja thali, adorning it with a candle or diya, an assortment of sweets, matthi, and a pot filled with water.

- Women reverently set up a large plate, positioning a candle/diya and incense in front of an image/statue of Goddess Parvati, symbolizing her unwavering marital devotion and formidable strength.
- Molis are tied around wrists, and Tikas are lovingly applied to each other's foreheads.
- The sacred narrative of Karwa Chauth is solemnly recounted, either by a priest or an esteemed elder, or transmitted through radio broadcasts, internet streaming platforms like YouTube, or by eloquent oral delivery from a cherished text.

The Festival Stories

The highlight of the afternoon is the captivating story of Karva Chauth when women gather at home or at a temple and hear the story. The story revolves around the unwavering love and sacrifice of a woman who successfully revived her husband from the clutches of death through her devotion and faith. This poignant tale is a powerful reminder of marital commitment and the unwavering strength of love.

The Enchanting Tale of Veeravati

The story of Karva Chauth revolves around a beautiful queen named Veeravati, known for her unwavering love and devotion to her husband, the king. As tradition dictates, Veeravati observed her first Karva Chauth after her marriage by diligently following the strict fast.

However, the queen couldn't bear the hunger pains due to her delicate constitution. By evening, Veeravati was too weak and fainted. Now, the queen had seven brothers who loved her dearly. They couldn't stand the plight of their sister and decided to end her fast by deceiving her. They made a fire at the nearby hill, creating a shimmering glow. Deceiving their sister, they claimed it was the moonlight reflecting off the night sky, signaling the perfect time to break the fast. Believing their words, the innocent Veeravati partook in a meal, unknowingly breaking the vows of her fast.

However, when the queen ate her dinner, she received the news that her husband was dead. The queen was heartbroken and rushed to her husband's palace. On the way, she met God Shiva and his consort, Goddess Parvati. Parvati informed her that the king had died because the queen had broken her fast by watching a false moon. However, when the queen asked her for forgiveness, Parvati granted her the boon that the king would be revived but would be ill. She also would have to do the Karwa Chauth fasts with strict rituals, faith and devotion.

Energized by this second chance, Veeravati reached the palace. She found the king lying unconscious with hundreds of needles inserted in his body. Each day, the queen removed one needle from the king's body. Next year, on the day of Karva Chauth, only one needle remained embedded in the body of the unconscious king.

The queen observed a strict fast that day, and when she went to the market to buy the karva for the puja, her maid removed the remaining needle from the king's body. Overwhelmed with joy at his revival, he showered his affection on the wrong woman. Veeravati, the true queen, was relegated to the role of a servant in her own palace.

Despite this cruel twist of fate, Veeravati never wavered. Her devotion to her husband and faith in the Karva Chauth rituals remained unshakeable. Every year, she continued to observe the fast with utmost dedication.

One day, when the king was going to some other kingdom, he asked Veeravati, the real queen (who had now turned maid), if she wanted anything. The queen asked for a pair of identical dolls. The king obliged, and the queen kept singing, " Roli ki Goli ho gayi... Goli ki Roli ho gayi " (the queen has turned into a maid, and the maid has become a queen).

On being asked by the king as to why she kept repeating that song, Veeravati narrated the entire story. The king repented and restored the queen to her royal status. The queen's devotion and faith won her husband's affection and the blessings of Goddess Parvati.

After Story Rituals

1. Women offer prayers for their husband's well-being, marital happiness, and the enduring harmony of their relationship.

2. Women engage in a ritual of unity and camaraderie by passing and exchanging their meticulously decorated thalis (plates) seven times within a circle of fellow women, accompanied by chanting the traditional Karva Chauth song. The ambiance is enhanced with the melodious rendition of the music playing softly in the background, either sourced from any available medium or simply through heartfelt intention.

3. Women extend Baiya, a symbolic offering, to their revered Mother-In-law. In cases where the mother-in-law is not present, the Baiya is graciously presented to a representative from the husband's side of the family, an esteemed elder within the household, a cherished friend, or a beloved sister.

4. Women partake in a moment of enjoying tea and water while invoking the blessings of Goddess Parvati for the strength and fortitude to sustain their fast until the auspicious moment of moonrise.

Karva Chauth song while exchanging thalis

"Veero Kudiye Karwada,

Sarv Suhagan Karwada,

A Katti Na Ateri Naa,

Kumbh Chrakhra Feri Naa,

Gwand Pair payeen Naa,

Sui Che Dhaga Payeen Naa

Ruthda maniyen Naa,

Suthra Jagayeen Naa,

Bhain Pyari Veeran,

Chan Chade Te Pani Peena

Ve Veero Kuriye Karwara,

Ve Sarv Suhagan Karwara.

This song highlights the things women should avoid while fasting. It mentions that women should not weave clothes, try to please anyone who is upset, or awaken someone who is sleeping. When the fast is over, these restrictions are lifted, and women can freely resume these activities along with others that were prohibited during the fast.

Evening Of Karwa Chauth

As the evening approaches, women cook special meals with love and devotion, preparing dishes to be enjoyed once the fast is broken. The meal consists of rice, lentils, and vegetables.

Night of Karwa Chauth, Fast Breaking Ritual

When the Moon Rises, it's time to break the fast with decorated thalis and lit candles.

- Women participate in a sacred ritual, singing hymns and setting heartfelt intentions as they offer water seven times from the pot to the radiant Moon.
- Women offer matthi to the luminous Moon seven times, symbolizing their dedication and supplication.
- Women devotionally gaze at the moon and then their loving husbands through sieves, a symbolic act reflecting their enduring love and devotion.
- Women offer prayers beseeching blessings upon their marital union, invoking divine grace for enduring harmony and bliss.

Following the culmination of the fast, women joyfully partake in a celebratory feast with their beloved husbands and cherished—family members. The precious moments of togetherness are immortalized through the lens, capturing the essence of love and unity in beautiful photographs and videos.

Song During Breaking Fast

Sir Dhadi,

Paer Kadi,

Ark Dendi,

Sarv Suhagan,

Chaubare Khadi.

The song depicts a married woman concluding her Karwa Chauth fast by offering 'ark' to the moon. It symbolizes the successful completion of her fast, which is observed for the well-being and longevity of her marriage.

The Festival Legacy

Karwa Chauth is a simple yet profound testament to enduring love, akin to a beautiful love story. The day's traditions deepen our bond and strengthen our commitment. Passing on this tradition to future generations allows us to share stories of devotion and celebrate the essence of our relationships.

Dusshera/Dashera/Vijayadashami

The Festival Calendar

"Dussehra" is derived from the Sanskrit words "Dasha," meaning ten, and "hara," meaning defeat, which together signifies the triumph of Lord Ram over the demon king Ravan, as depicted in the Hindu epic, the Ramayana. According to the English calendar, it comes in October, and as per the Hindu Calendar, Dussehra falls on the 10th day of the Sharad Navratri festival. This alignment with Navratri highlights the concept of Durga Puja, a celebration of the Goddess Durga, who victoriously kills the demons and empowers Lord Ram in his battle against Ravan.

The Festival Stories

Once upon a time, a powerful and intelligent king named Ravan lived in a kingdom, Lanka. Despite his strength, Ravan's heart became consumed by arrogance, and he began to misuse his powers, causing suffering to his subjects.

The Gods, witnessing the suffering caused by Ravan, decided to intervene. God Vishnu took on the avatar of Prince Ram as the son of a wise and beloved king named Dasharath in the ancient city of Ayodhya. Ram was a noble prince who held a special place in the hearts of the people for his kindness and righteousness.

However, a twist of fate led Dasharath's youngest queen, Kaikeyi, to demand that her son, Bharat, be crowned as the heir to the throne. Influenced by her maid Manthara, Kaikeyi's decision forced Lord

Ram into exile for fourteen years, breaking the hearts of the people who adored him.

Devastated but undeterred, Ram, his devoted wife Sita, and loyal brother Lakshman set out into the unknown. The story takes another turn when Ravan, enchanted by Sita's beauty, kidnaps her and takes her to his kingdom of Lanka. Determined to rescue his beloved wife, Prince Ram seeks the help of a diverse army of monkeys led by the courageous Lord Hanuman. Together, they face numerous challenges and overcome obstacles to reach Lanka.

In a final showdown, Ram faces Ravan in a fierce battle. With the blessings of the Goddess Durga and the help of friends and family, Ram defeats Ravan in a long battle and restores peace to the kingdom. Dusshera is also celebrated for Goddess Durga's victory over all demons, including Mahishasura.

Dussehra, or Vijayadashami, is celebrated to honor this victory of good over evil. People light lamps, share sweets, and come together for festive events to commemorate the triumph of kindness, love, and justice. It's a time for joyous celebration, symbolizing the human spirit's victory over life's challenges.

The Festival Celebration "Step by Step"

Dussehra marks the culmination of Sharad Navratri, a nine-day festival filled with enthusiasm and devotion. During Dussehra, we utilize the leaves of barley/ Jo/or wheatgrass, which were ceremoniously sown and nurtured in cow dung in traditional Indian customs or the soil in Western practices throughout Sharad Navratri. These vibrant green leaves signify auspiciousness and abundance, reflecting our aspirations for prosperity.

Prepare for the Festival and Perform the Puja

Embrace the spirit of Dussehra by cleansing yourself with a refreshing shower. Offer a Puja and follow the steps of "How to Perform Puja," as outlined in the Puja chapter. If time is limited, follow the steps of "A Simple Daily Puja" with a simple prayer as described under "Puja and Prayer Methods."

NOTE: Immerse the Sanjhi Mata (Goddess Durga Avatar) in flowing water. (if you have made Sanjhi Mata artwork during Sharad Navratri)

Brother/Sister Blessing Ritual: *For Those Who Sowed Barley/Jau/ Wheat-grass During Sharad Navratri.*

Ritual Performed by Sister: Carefully pluck the Barley/Jau /Wheatgrass leaves grown during Sharad Navratri. Tuck the leaves behind their brothers' ears or on their caps, symbolizing good luck and seeking Lord Ram's blessings for righteousness and Goddess Durga's protection. If seeds weren't sowed, offer Tika, Moli, and sweets to your brother.

Ritual Performed by Brother: Reciprocate with gifts/money as a token of gratitude to sisters.

Conclude with Blessings Ritual

After the ritual, the brothers wear the leaves for some time, which is believed to bring luck and prosperity. Later, some leaves are consumed with food, while some are thrown during Rath Yatras (Lord Ram Parade) in India, and finally, some are kept in a safe locker in red cloth for blessings until the next Navratri.

Participate and Celebrate Community Festivities

- Enjoy local events and fairs in your area during the festival. Watch a lively play called Ram Lila, which tells the story of Lord Ram and his adventures.

- Participate in temple and community events, such as burning effigies of Ravan and his brothers, which symbolize the rejection of negative qualities.
- Be sure to capture the festival's beauty by taking pictures so you can celebrate, enjoy, and remember the moments together.
- Learn more about Dussehra by reading or watching the Ramayana story. It's a great way to understand why we celebrate this festival.

As Dusshera concludes, the victory of good over evil and the joyful festivities become sweet memories. The celebrations bid us farewell, leaving a sense of positivity and triumph.

The Festival Legacy

Celebrating Dussehra is not just a tradition; it's a vibrant reminder that goodness triumphs over negativity. As we witness the effigies burn and chant "Jai Shri Ram," let us also commit to burning away negativity within ourselves and fostering the light of goodness in our hearts. As we partake in these festivities, let's cherish the importance of passing down these celebrations to the next generation to ensure that the values of the victory of good over evil remain alive.

Diwali/ Deepawali

Diwali, also called Deepawali, means rows of lights. This vibrant five-day Hindu festival is celebrated in October/November, with each day having its particular significance and ceremony. In this chapter, we'll take a closer look at each day of Diwali and find out why it's so special. So, let's dive into the excitement of Diwali, step by step, and discover the stories and traditions that make this "Festival of Lights" so much fun!

Day 1: Dhanteras

Day 2: Naraka Chaturdashi - Choti Diwali

Day 3: Diwali- The Main Celebration of Diwali

Day 4: Govardhan Puja

Day 5: Bhai Dooj

Dhanteras – the Beginning of Diwali

The Festival Calendar

Dhanteras is associated with the God Dhanvantari, the God of Ayurveda Medicine. The word "Dhanteras" is derived from two Sanskrit words: "Dhan," which means wealth, and "Teras," which refers to the thirteenth lunar day. Dhanteras is celebrated on the thirteenth day of the Krishna Paksha (waning phase of the moon) in Kartik, which usually falls in October or November. It marks the beginning of the Diwali festival, a significant Hindu celebration.

The Festival Stories

One popular story associated with Dhanteras is primarily linked to the legend of the churning of the cosmic ocean (Samudra Manthan) found in Hindu scripts. The narrative involves the Gods (devas) and the mischievous demons (asuras) working together to churn the ocean, using a giant mountain, Mount Mandara, as the churning rod and Vasuki, a massive serpent, for a rope!

During this churning, various divine beings and treasures emerged from the ocean depths. One significant element surfacing was the pot of amrita, the elixir of immortality. Of course, the demons wanted to keep it all for themselves and managed to seize the pot, leading to a celestial tug-of-war between the Gods and demons for this magical potion.

Amid the chaos, a divine figure appeared: Dhanvantari, an incarnation of God Vishnu (the physician of the Gods). He emerged, holding a pot of amrita and a book on Ayurveda. Dhavantari's arrival tipped the scales in favor of the Gods, symbolizing the triumph of good over evil and the restoration of balance.

Another Tale of Light and Luck

In addition, Dhanteras is also associated with another popular story about a wise King named Hima. His son was destined to be bitten by a snake on the fourth day of his marriage, a prophecy that surely filled the kingdom with worry.

The new bride, a clever princess determined to save her husband, devised a brilliant plan. So, on the fourth night, she stacked all their shiny jewelry and coins at the entrance to their home and lit countless lamps. She then kept her husband awake throughout the night with stories and fun activities.

When Yama, the God of Death, arrived as a snake, he was mesmerized by the dazzling display of light and wealth. He becomes so engrossed in the scene that he stays all night listening to the princess's stories, forgetting his mission to claim the prince's life.

By sunrise, Yama had to leave without harming the prince. The princess's bright plan saved her husband, and the kingdom was filled with happiness. Since then, people have celebrated this day by lighting lamps and putting out shiny things on Dhanteras.

The Festival Celebration "Step by Step"

Dhanteras holds a special place in the hearts of those who seek healing, prosperity, and blessings. Let's dive into the simple and happy traditions that make Dhanteras a time of joy and plenty.

Prepare for the Festival

Start by thoroughly cleaning your home. A fresh and sparkling space welcomes good vibes and sets the stage for the festivities. Wear traditional clothing as a symbolic gesture to appreciate Hindu traditions.

Invest in Gold, Silver Coins, and Shiny Kitchen Utensils

Consider buying a small gold or silver coin for good luck and prosperity. Invest in some sparkling new kitchen utensils to attract good fortune. These precious metals and utensils are supposed to attract wealth and fortune in the coming year.

Seek Blessings

Take a moment to offer prayers and seek blessings from God Dhanvantari for the health and well-being of you and your loved ones. As you participate in these traditions, pause, appreciate their significance, and feel grateful for the good things in your life.

Cherish the moments

Don't forget to capture precious memories by taking numerous pictures, sharing the experience with your family, and sowing the seeds of curiosity and significance among them. Encourage everyone's participation and foster the continuation of this cherished tradition.

The Festival Legacy

As Dhanteras concludes, our homes shine with cleanliness, the glow of new treasures, and the blessings of good health. From cleaning up to getting gold or silver and seeking blessings from God Dhanvantari, each step adds joy and positivity. With gratitude, we step into Diwali, carrying the warmth of Dhanteras into the festivities ahead.

Naraka Chaturdashi (Choti Diwali)

The Festival Calendar

The vibrant tapestry of Diwali unfolds, and day two brings us to Naraka Chaturdashi, also known as Choti Diwali (Little Diwali). This special day holds a story of epic battles, brave heroes, and the ultimate victory of good over evil.

"Naraka Chaturdashi" is a beautiful combination of two words: "Naraka," referring to the demon Narakasura, who wreaked havoc on the world. "Chaturdashi" signifies the fourteenth day of the lunar fortnight. This day symbolizes the victory of good over evil and light over darkness. The name encapsulates the essence of the day's celebration, marking the defeat of negativity and the triumph of positive forces.

The Festival Stories

Once upon a time, a powerful and wicked demon named Narakasura ruled with an iron fist. He terrorized the world and captured many innocent beings. The people, weary of his tyranny, yearned for peace and freedom. Their fervent prayers reached the ears of Lord Krishna.

Lord Krishna, touched by the plight of the people, confronted Narakasura in a fierce battle. After a challenging fight, Lord Krishna defeated the demon and liberated the captive souls. Before his defeat, Narakasura, shaken to his core, realized the consequences of his actions and sought forgiveness. This moment of remorse signifies the possibility of redemption, a message that resonates deeply within the celebration of Naraka Chaturdashi.

As a symbol of triumph over evil, the day when Lord Krishna defeated Narakasura came to be celebrated as Naraka Chaturdashi or Choti Diwali. It represents the victory of goodness and light, bringing joy and hope to all.

The Festival Celebration "Step by Step"

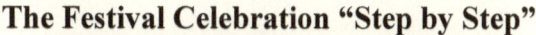

When the sun announces Naraka Chaturdashi, a day symbolizing the triumph of light, embrace the simple traditions that carry cultural and spiritual significance.

Prepare for the Festival

As the first rays of dawn paint the sky, greet Naraka Chaturdashi with a refreshing cleansing routine. Bathe or shower, washing away negativity and preparing your body and mind for the festivities. Embrace the festive spirit by wearing traditional clothes that reflect the cultural richness of the day. A vibrant sari for women, a comfortable dhoti for men, or even a kurta can add a special touch to the occasion.

Offer Puja to Lord Krishna

Engage in a serene meditation or offer heartfelt prayers to Krishna, infusing your morning with spiritual devotion. Follow the steps of "How to Perform Puja," as outlined in the Puja chapter, taking the time to understand the meaning and purpose behind each ritual. If time is limited, follow the steps of "A Simple Daily Puja" with a simple prayer as described under "Puja and Prayer Methods.".

Spread the Light

As dusk settles, illuminate your home by placing lamps or diyas (oil lamps). These flickering flames symbolize the dispelling of lingering shadows and inviting positivity into every corner.

Cherish the Moments

Take numerous pictures to capture precious memories. Share the experience with your loved ones, especially children, explaining the story behind Naraka Chaturdashi. Through these shared moments, you nurture the festival's spirit and ensure its continuation for future generations.

The Festival Legacy

Naraka Chaturdashi not only honors our rich cultural heritage but also reinforces the enduring values of hope, unity, and the triumph of good over evil, creating lasting memories and traditions that are passed down through generations. By embracing these cherished customs, Naraka Chaturdashi becomes a radiant chapter in our festive legacy.

अ

Diwali

The Festival Calendar

Welcome to the heart of Diwali. Day 3 of our Diwali exploration brings us to the heart of the festival – Diwali Day or Lakshmi Puja. Diwali, also called Deepawali, means rows of lights. This special day is dedicated to the worship of Goddess Lakshmi, who brings prosperity and light. It's also a day to remember Lord Ram's return to Ayodhya, a tale of triumph over darkness. Let's learn the enchanting celebration of Diwali Day, where lamps glow, prayers abound, and the spirit of abundance fills the air.

The Festival Stories

Legends abound surrounding Diwali. One tale takes us back to a time known as Treta Yuga, where gods and demons joined forces to churn the ocean for the elixir of immortality. From the churning ocean emerged many treasures, and among them was the radiant Goddess Lakshmi. Clad in stunning attire and adorned with exquisite jewels, she captivated everyone with her beauty. Recognizing the virtue and goodness of God Vishnu, she chooses Vishnu as her eternal companion.

On Diwali Day, it is believed that Goddess Lakshmi and his consort God Vishnu visit well-lit and clean homes, showering them with blessings of prosperity and abundance. Devotees prepare for Goddess Lakshmi's arrival by cleaning their homes, lighting lamps, and creating intricate rangoli designs at their doorsteps to welcome the goddess of wealth.

Another captivating story narrates that a wise and beloved king named Dasharath lived in the ancient city of Ayodhya. His eldest son, Ram (the incarnation of God Vishnu/Narayan), was a noble prince who held a special place in the hearts of the people for his kindness and righteousness.

However, a twist of fate led Dasharath's youngest queen, Kaikeyi, to demand that her son, Bharat, be crowned as the heir to the throne. Influenced by her maid Manthara, Kaikeyi's decision forced Lord Ram into exile for fourteen years, breaking the hearts of the people who adored him.

Devastated but undeterred, Ram, his devoted wife Sita, and loyal brother Lakshman set out into the unknown. Their journey during exile was filled with obstacles, but they found allies in unexpected places, including the mighty monkey Lord, Hanuman.

Meanwhile, in the island kingdom of Lanka, the demon king Ravan, driven by greed and power, abducted Sita. This act sparked a fierce battle as Ram, with the help of Hanuman and a courageous army of monkeys, waged war against Ravan to rescue his beloved wife.

The epic battle concluded with Ram's victory over Ravan on the auspicious day of Dusshera/Vijayadashami. The triumphant return of Ram, Sita, and Lakshman to Ayodhya marked the beginning of Diwali celebrations. Citizens, overwhelmed with joy, illuminated the city with rows of lamps, symbolizing the victory of light over darkness.

The Festival Celebration "Step by Step"

Diwali is a day filled with light, prayers, and family gatherings. Let's follow some easy steps to celebrate Diwali Day with joy and tradition.

Diwali Checklist

- Colors for Rangoli or Readymade Rangoli

- Gifts for Family Members

- Clay/Brass/Copper Idols/Statues of deities Lakshmi, Ram and Ganesh

- Hatadi (House of Gods) made of Silver or Clay with built-in idols (optional)

- Oil lamps/candles

- Incense sticks or Dhoop

- Fresh flowers and Fruits

- Yummy sweets

- Game Tambola or Bingo

- Fireworks if allowed

The Morning of Diwali

- Begin by taking a refreshing shower and feeling the cool water wash away any tiredness. Put on traditional clothes, letting the vibrant colors add a touch of festive elegance to your day.

- Visit your family and friends, sharing smiles and exchanging thoughtful sweets and gifts. Feel the joy of togetherness as you connect with your loved ones.

- Stroll through vibrant markets, shops, and temples, soaking in the enchanting decorations that adorn the surroundings. Let the festive atmosphere fill your heart with wonder and delight.

The Afternoon/Evening of Diwali

- As the evening approaches, prepare for the special prayer time. Create a sacred space, adorning it with decorations that evoke a sense of divine presence.

- Express your creativity by crafting colorful Rangoli designs at the entrance of your home. Each intricate pattern shall tell a story of beauty and tradition.

- Engage in mindful entertainment with games like Tambola or Bingo with a small stake. Let the laughter and friendly competition create an atmosphere of joy, adding a playful touch to the evening.

- Enjoy visiting a local temple and offering Ghee Diyas, fruits, flowers, and other offerings to Goddess Lakshmi and God Vishnu.

The Night of Diwali

Ganesh Puja

Read and perform step-by-step Puja from chapter Puja with an intention. If time is limited, follow the steps of "A Simple Daily Puja" with a simple prayer as described under "Puja and Prayer Methods."

- Light oil lamps throughout your home to create a warm, inviting space.
- Begin your Puja ceremony by offering prayers to Lord Ganesh for new beginnings and removing obstacles. Seek his blessings for a smooth and auspicious start to your Diwali puja.

Lakshmi Puja: The Heart of Diwali

- Place sweets in the temple or Hatadi (House of Gods) as an offering to Laxmi, Vishnu, and Ganesh.
- Chant and say prayers to Goddess Lakshmi, seeking her blessings for prosperity, good fortune, and happiness.
- Conclude the Puja with an Arti to Goddess Lakshmi and God Vishnu (Narayan).

Kindly note that the prayers, chants, and Arti for the Ganesh and Lakshmi Puja can be played in the background to enhance the spiritual atmosphere.

Meditate & Seek Blessings

Take a quiet moment to meditate. Focus your thoughts on success, positivity, and gratitude for all the blessings in your life. Remember the core values of Diwali – be thankful for what you have, appreciate all the good things in life, and extend kindness to others. Let the spirit of Diwali inspire you to cultivate positivity and gratitude in your heart.

Light up the Fireworks (if permitted) or in the Temple

Light up the night sky with dazzling fireworks, adhering to local regulations to ensure safety. Enjoy the bright bursts of color that symbolize the triumph of light over darkness. If fireworks are not permitted in your area, you can enjoy the fireworks activities in your local temples.

Enjoy the Grand Feast

Celebrate the day with a delicious and festive meal shared with loved ones. Savor the unique flavors of traditional Diwali dishes and take a moment to appreciate the joyous occasion.

Cherish the moments

Capture precious moments of your Diwali celebration with photographs. Share this special experience with your family and friends, fostering a sense of curiosity and appreciation for the significance of this cherished tradition. Encourage everyone's participation to ensure these customs thrive for generations to come.

Ganesh Puja Prayer

Vakr tunda Maha kaya Surya koti Sama prabha

Nir vighnam Kuru Me Deva Sarva-Kaary eshu Sarvada

This prayer invokes Lord Ganesh, the remover of obstacles and the God of wisdom and beginnings. The prayer praises Ganesh's magnificence and seeks his blessings to remove hindrances and ensure success in all endeavours.

Lakshmi Puja Prayer

Om Jai Laxmi Mata, Maiya Jai Laxmi Mata, Tumko nis din sevat, Har, Vishnu Dhata, Om Jai Laxmi Mata.

Uma Rama Brahmaani, Tum ho Jag Mata, Maiya Tum hi Jag Mata,

Surya ChanRam dhyaavat, Naarad Rishi gaata. Om Jai Laxmi Mata.

Durga Roop Niranjani, Sukh Sampati Data, Maiya Sukh Sampati Data,

Jo koyee tumko dhyaataa, Ridhee Sidhee dhan paataa .Om Jai Laxmi Mata.

Tum pataal Nivasani, Tum hi Shubh Daataa || Maiya Tum hi Shubh Daataa.

Karm prabhav prakasini, Bhav-nidhi kit rata !! Om Jai Laxmi Mata.

Jis ghar mein tum rehtee, sab sad-gun aataa, Maiya sab sad-gun aataa.

Sab sambhav ho jaata, Man naheen ghabraataa. Om Jai Laxmi Mata.

Tum bin Yagna na hote, Vastra na ho pata, Maiya , Vastra na ho pata.

Khan Paan ka vaibhav, Sab tumase aata ! Om Jai Laxmi Mata.

Subh gun mandir sundar, kshirodadhi jaata, Maiya kshirodadhi jaata.

Ratna chaturdash tum bin, koi nahi paata! Om Jai Laxmi Mata.

Maha Laxmiji ki aarati, Jo koi jan gaata, Maiya jo koi jan gaata.

Ur anand samaata, paap utar jaata ! Om Jai Laxmi Mata.

This is a devotional prayer to Goddess Lakshmi, celebrating her divine qualities and invoking her blessings. It begins with a call for victory to Lakshmi, acknowledging her as the consort of Vishnu and the creator of all, who is worshipped day and night. The hymn reveres Lakshmi as Uma, Rama, and Brahmani, embodying various divine aspects and being the mother of the world, adored by celestial beings like the Sun, Moon, and sage Narada. Lakshmi is also recognized as an embodiment of Durga, the goddess who grants happiness and wealth. Those who meditate upon her are blessed -

with success, fulfillment, and wealth. Singing this prayer brings happiness, bliss, and liberation from sins, highlighting the transformative power of devotion to Goddess Lakshmi.

The Festival Legacy

Diwali's enduring legacy lies in its universal themes of renewal and joy. It brings people together in celebration and goodwill and holds deep cultural and spiritual significance. Diwali is a beacon of hope, encouraging the pursuit of righteousness and the dispelling of darkness, making it a cherished festival for millions worldwide.

Govardhan Puja (Annakut)

The Festival Calendar

As we delve deeper into Diwali festivities, Day 4 brings us Govardhan Puja. The name "Govardhan Puja" is derived from two components: "Govardhan," referring to the Govardhan Hill, and "Puja," which means worship or reverence. This day is also known as "Annakut," where "Anna" means food and "Kut" means heap. Together, Govardhan Puja signifies the worship and reverence offered to Govardhan Hill, primarily associated with Lord Krishna's divine act of lifting the hill to protect the people of Vrindavan. The day also involves making offerings of various foods, expressing gratitude for the abundance provided by nature and the protective grace of Lord Krishna.

The Festival Stories

Long ago, in Vrindavan, a small village nestled amidst rolling hills, lived the people who worshipped Lord Indra, the god of rain. They believed his blessings were essential for bountiful harvests and a prosperous life. However, young Krishna, known for his wisdom and divine connection, proposed a different approach. He suggested that the villagers shift their reverence to Govardhan Hill, a majestic landmark that provided fertile soil for their crops, grazing lands for their cows, and a sense of security.

Lord Indra, displeased with this change in tradition, sent a torrential downpour upon Vrindavan, aiming to punish the villagers for their defiance. In response, Krishna lifted Govardhan Hill with the little finger of his hand, creating a giant, natural umbrella that sheltered the villagers and their livestock from the relentless rain. Krishna held the hill aloft for seven days and nights until Lord Indra finally conceded defeat and withdrew the storm.

Witnessing Krishna's divine powers, the villagers understood the true source of their protection. In gratitude, they began to worship Govardhan Hill. Since then, Govardhan Puja has been celebrated to honor the love and care that Lord Krishna showed to the people of Vrindavan and to express gratitude for the bountiful gifts of nature.

The Festival Celebration "Step by Step"

Let's embrace the traditional significance of this day, which is marked by gratitude for nature's abundance. In the West, we convey our gratitude to Lord Krishna for the abundant food through sincere prayer. We acknowledge the plenty and seek divine protection, recognizing that resources are comparatively limited here as opposed to in India. In India, there's a special tradition where people create a symbolic hill using cow dung, decorate it with flowers, and load it with various food offerings for Krishna. They call it "Annakut," or a mountain of food. As part of the ritual, people walk around this symbolic hill, expressing gratitude and seeking blessings.

While geographical distance might separate you from traditional Indian celebrations, the core message of Govardhan Puja, appreciating nature's bounty and expressing gratitude, transcends borders. Here's how you can celebrate this meaningful day in your own unique way.

Perform Traditional Puja

Offer a traditional Puja and follow the steps of "How to Perform Puja," as outlined in the Puja chapter, taking the time to understand the meaning and purpose behind each ritual. If time is limited, follow the steps of "A Simple Daily Puja" with a simple prayer as described under "Puja and Prayer Methods."

Enjoy the Vegetarian Feast

Cook and share a tasty vegetarian meal to share with loved ones. This vegetarian focus reflects the traditional offerings made to Govardhan Hill. Savor the flavors and appreciate the nourishment provided by nature.

Connect with Nature

Take a walk in the park, visit a local farmers market, or simply appreciate the beauty of your surroundings. Reconnect with nature and acknowledge its importance in our lives.

Share, Tell, and Cherish

Extend the celebration by sharing food with others. Organize or donate community meals to spread gratitude. Don't forget to capture precious memories by taking numerous pictures, sharing the experience with your family, and sowing the seeds of curiosity and significance among them. Encourage everyone's participation and foster the continuation of this cherished tradition.

The Festival Legacy

Govardhan Puja is more than just a religious festival; it's a beautiful reminder of our deep connection with nature and the importance of expressing gratitude. As we celebrate this day, let's embrace the lessons it imparts – to cherish the environment, appreciate the abundance that surrounds us, and cultivate a spirit of thankfulness for the life-sustaining gifts of nature.

Bhai Dooj

The Festival Calendar

Welcome to Bhai Dooj, a heartwarming celebration nestled within the festive spirit of the final day of Diwali. "Bhai" refers to brother, and "Dooj" means the second day after the new moon, usually in late October or early November. This special day radiates the essence of love and familial bonds, specifically focusing on the unique connection between brothers and sisters.

The Festival Stories

Bhai Dooj is a cherished celebration that beautifully symbolizes the profound connection between brothers and sisters. This day is rooted in ancient legends, with tales embodying love, protection, and timeless bonds.

One such legend revolves around Lord Krishna and his sister Subhadra. After vanquishing a demon, Krishna visited Subhadra, who warmly welcomed him by applying a tilak on his forehead and offering him delicious sweets. In this joyful exchange, Krishna blessed Subhadra, deepening their bond as they exchanged heartfelt gifts and created cherished memories.

Another story tells of Yamraj, the God of death, who was separated from his sister Yamuna due to his duties in the netherworld. Yamuna, yearning to reunite with her brother, prayed to Lord Krishna to meet her brother again. Moved by Yamuna's sincerity, Krishna facilitated a reunion between the siblings.

Overjoyed to be reunited, Yamraj and Yamuna embraced each other affectionately. Yamuna adorned Yamraj's forehead with a tilak and performed arti, expressing her love and devotion. Yamraj promised to visit Yamuna every year on Bhai Dooj to renew their bond and express his affection. He also declared that whoever performs rituals for their brothers on this day, along with sharing meals prepared by their sisters, will be protected from fear of death. Additionally, he pledged to release souls from hell, bringing liberation to all. Bhai Dooj, therefore, stands as a testament to the enduring bonds between siblings, where love, rituals, and stories intertwine to create a celebration that transcends time.

<h3 style="text-align:center">The Festival Celebration "Step by Step"</h3>

During Bhai Dooj, we commemorate the cherished bond between brothers and sisters. Before delving into the festivities, let's take a moment to prepare for the celebration and bask in the warmth and joy that the festival brings.

Bhai Dooj Checklist

- Puja Thali: To hold offerings and items
- Diya/Lamp/Candle and Lighter: For lighting during the Puja
- Incense Sticks/Dhoop: To create a fragrant atmosphere
- Moli/Sacred Thread: For tying around the wrist

- Tilak: To apply on the Forehead
- Grains of Rice: For applying on tilak
- Fruits, Sweets, or Home-Made Prasad: To express gratitude.
- Gift/Money for Sister: A token of appreciation for your sister's love and support.
- Sweets for Brother: Sweet treats to show your brother your love and care.

Now, Let's embark on the sacred & joyous journey, where every step is filled with devotion and sincerity.

Prepare for the Ceremony

Before diving into the festivities of Bhai Dooj, cleanse yourself with a refreshing shower and don traditional clothing to honor the occasion's cultural significance and add to the festive spirit.

Perform Traditional Puja

Do the traditional Puja in the home temple to Lord Krishna and Yamraj to grant protection, long life, and love between siblings. Follow the steps of "How to Perform Puja," as outlined in the Puja chapter, taking the time to understand the meaning and purpose behind each ritual. If time is limited, follow the steps of "A Simple Daily Puja" with a simple prayer as described under "Puja and Prayer Methods."

Perform Bhai Dooj Ritual (Sister)

- After Puja, use your right thumb to apply a tilak (vermilion mark) on your brother's forehead.

- Apply unbroken grains of rice on tilak.

- Tie the Moli on the Right hand, the sacred thread on the brother's wrist, as a symbol of protection and love.

- Wave a lit lamp in the Puja Thali clockwise, praying for your brother's well-being and longevity.

- Offer sweets to brother.

Perform Bhai Dooj Blessings Ritual (Brother)

After performing Bhai Dooj rituals, the brother offers tokens of love, such as money, gifts, etc., as a symbol of blessing to the sister. This exchange symbolizes the love and care shared between siblings and strengthens the familial bond.

Enjoy Feast and Happiness

After the rituals, sit down together and enjoy a delicious feast as a family. Sharing a meal is a way to celebrate the joyous occasion and foster unity and happiness within the family.

Capture Memories of Special Moments

Don't forget to capture these special moments by taking plenty of pictures to cherish the memories for years to come. These photographs are a beautiful reminder of the love and togetherness shared during the Bhai Dooj celebrations.

The Festival Legacy

Bhai Dooj is a special occasion that reminds us of the importance of looking out for one another and cherishing the joy of family bonds. For the younger generation, it's an opportunity to appreciate the uniqueness of sibling relationships and carry forward the tradition of expressing love and gratitude in a heartfelt, thoughtful manner.

Festival Notes

Use this space to track festival dates and record-keeping.

Use a pencil for easy adjustments and accuracy.

Chapter 9

Uncovering Subtle Festivities

Discovering Hindu significant days and festivals unveils a rich tapestry of celebrations and spiritual insights. Beyond Diwali, Holi, and other major festivals and days, there are lesser-celebrated but equally essential occasions. Each day carries unique traditions, symbolizing different aspects of life and spirituality. As we explore these less-known moments, we find a beautiful mosaic of culture and wisdom, fostering unity, compassion, and a deep appreciation for life's sacred beauty.

Makar Sakranti (Maghi)

Makar Sankranti, also known as Maghi or simply Sankranti, is a Hindu festival that marks the sun's transition into the zodiac sign of Capricorn (Makar Rashi). It typically falls on the 14th of January every year. This festival signifies the end of the winter solstice and the subsequent lengthening of days. However, the date may vary slightly depending on the Hindu calendar.

Celebrated widely across India, Makar Sankranti takes on a unique character in different regions, with diverse traditions and practices adding a delightful layer of cultural richness.

The sky comes alive with vibrant hues as people fly kites, share sweets like til laddus (sesame seed sweets), savour traditional kheer (rice pudding), and participate in vibrant fairs and cultural events. Some take a holy dip in rivers like the Ganges or Yamuna, seeking blessings and purification. Prayers are offered to the sun god for prosperity. Communities organize fairs and cultural events to celebrate this joyful time, marking the start of longer days.

Sheetala Ashtami Mata Puja/Basoda/Basdiya Puja

Sheetala Ashtami, also known as Basoda/Basdiya, typically falls in the month of Chaitra (March-April) in the Hindu calendar and is dedicated to Sheetala Mata, the goddess associated with health and protection from diseases.

The worship of Sheetala Mata subtly emphasizes the importance of hygiene and preventative measures in maintaining good health. The celebration is scientifically significant due to seasonal health impacts. As winter transitions to summer, skin issues arise. On this day, people visit temples or set up home altars to pray and seek the goddess's blessings for good health and protection against ailments, especially fever and skin issues. Cooler foods like Pua and halwa are preferred. Only food prepared a day before is consumed before offering to Sheetla Mata on the celebration day.

Naag Panchami

Naag Panchami is a Hindu festival dedicated to the worship of snakes or serpents. It falls on the fifth day (Panchami) of the bright half of the lunar month of Shravana, usually in July or August.

Naag Panchami honors snakes, revered as divine beings in Hinduism. Snakes, often depicted with a wise and powerful aura, symbolize fertility, protection, and the potent energy of nature. This day marks Lord Krishna's victory over the serpent Kaliya, who terrorized the villagers of Gokul. However, the story goes beyond mere conquest. After defeating Kaliya, Lord Krishna, known for his compassion, spares the serpent's life, reminding him to use his power for good. Lord Krishna takes a promise from Kaliya that no snake should harm the people of Gokul. Devotees visit serpent temples, offering milk, sweets, flowers, and turmeric to idols or representations of snakes. Some communities even make offerings of milk at anthills, acknowledging the vital role snakes play in the ecosystem. The celebration underscores the symbolic importance of respecting nature and coexisting with animals, emphasizing family traditions, devotion, and the cultural significance of snakes in Hindu beliefs.

Sharad Purnima

Sharad Purnima, celebrated in October, marks the culmination of the harvest season and the gentle transition into autumn. It's a time for gratitude for the abundance nature provides. According to Hindu beliefs, on this night, the moon's rays are believed to contain medicinal properties and are beneficial for health. Devotees, particularly women, offer prayers to Goddess Lakshmi for prosperity, staying awake to sing and pray together. Families gather under the moonlit sky. People also remember the playful deeds of Lord Krishna, who danced with the Gopis in a divine celebration. In a remarkable act of unity, God Shiva himself took the form of Gopīśvara Mahādevā to join this joyous dance.

In this spirit of togetherness, families share meals made from the season's fresh produce, laughing and celebrating the joys of the harvest season. It's a time of unity, gratitude, and cherished moments spent under the benevolent light of the moon.

Kartika Purnima

Kartika Purnima is a Hindu festival celebrated on the full moon day in late October or early November. The festival commemorates the victory of good over evil, especially God Shiva's triumph over the demon Tripurasura. Kartika Purnima is also celebrated as the manifestation day of Matsya, the God Vishnu's fish incarnation (avatar). As dawn breaks, devotees rise early for ceremonial baths in rivers or sacred water bodies, symbolizing inner purification and washing away negativity. Rows of diyas (earthen lamps) are lit, casting a warm glow and illuminating the night sky. Prayers and religious chants fill the air, invoking blessings and expressing gratitude. Some devotees observe a fast or engage in charity to deepen their spiritual connection.

Tulsi Vivah (Marriage)

Tulsi is considered a sacred plant, revered for its divine and medicinal properties and is considered auspicious in Hindu households. According to the Hindu calendar, Tulsi Vivah is celebrated on the 12th day of the Shukla Paksha of the Kartik month.

The story of Tulsi Vivah centres on Vrinda, a devoted wife of the demon king Jalandhar. Although Jalandhar was evil, Vrinda's purity and faith protected him from defeat. Feeling threatened by his power, the gods sought Lord Vishnu's help. Vishnu took Jalandhar's form to deceive Vrinda, causing her to unknowingly break her chastity. As a result, Jalandhar was defeated by Lord Shiva. When Vrinda discovered the deception, she cursed Vishnu to become the black Shaligram stone. To honour her purity, Vishnu blessed her to be reborn as the sacred Tulsi plant, promising to marry her annually in this form. Thus, Tulsi Vivah is celebrated each year as the union of Lord Vishnu (in his Shaligram form) and the Tulsi plant. The marriage ceremony, often conducted in homes or temples, involves rituals, prayers, and offerings to sanctify the union.

Lesser-Known Celebrations

In addition to the ones mentioned above, several other observances hold significance for different communities. These are just a few examples of the many lesser-known Hindu celebrations that enrich the cultural landscape.

Pradosh Vrat: This day occurs twice a month on the 13th day of the waxing and waning lunar phases. Devotees fast, pray to God Shiva and Goddess Parvati, and visit temples for blessings.

Sankashti Chaturthi: Celebrated on the fourth day after the full moon, this occasion is dedicated to Lord Ganesh. Devotees seek his blessings for a smooth and successful journey through life.

Amavasya and Purnima: New moon (Amavasya) and full moon (Purnima) days are significant for religious observances, rituals, and prayers.

Guru Purnima: This is a day to honor and express gratitude to gurus or teachers, observed on the full moon in June-July.

Aja Ekadashi: This celebration, dedicated to God Vishnu, is held during the waxing phase of the moon in July/August. According to religious beliefs, all desires are fulfilled by observing a fast on the day of Aja Ekadashi.

NOTE: It is important to remember that some other dates and days hold more profound spiritual or religious significance for different communities. It's wise to seek the advice and guidance of elders when navigating such beliefs and practices, as they often carry centuries-old wisdom and traditions that can offer valuable insights into the significance and proper observance of these occasions.

Chapter 10

Understanding the Ancient Scriptures

Hinduism boasts a rich tapestry of sacred scriptures, each a cornerstone of its vast philosophical and spiritual landscape. These ancient texts, known collectively as Shastras, hold immense wisdom, guiding Hindus in their daily lives, spiritual practices, and understanding of the universe. In this chapter, we will highlight the basics of the scripture books.

Vedas

Vedas are the oldest scriptures and the foundation of Hinduism. The four divinely revealed texts—Rigveda, Samaveda, Yajurveda, and Atharvaveda are the base of Hindu philosophy, rituals, and theistic practices.

Rigveda: The "Book of Verses," the Rigveda is the oldest of the four Vedas and is a collection of hymns dedicated to various deities, including Agni (fire god), Indra (rain god), and Surya (sun god). It offers philosophical insights and explores themes of creation, sacrifice, and the relationship between humanity and the divine.

Samaveda: The "Book of Chants," the Samaveda consists primarily of melodies and chants (saman) derived from the Rigveda. These chants, integral to Vedic rituals, are sung by priests during religious ceremonies, adding a layer of musical beauty to the practice.

Yajurveda: The "Book of Sacrificial Formulas" the Yajurveda focuses on the practical aspects of rituals and sacrifices. It comprises a collection of prose mantras and verses used in rituals and sacrificial ceremonies, providing instructions for performing rituals.

Atharvaveda: The "Book of Spells" holds a unique position among the Vedas. It includes hymns, chants, and spells for healing, protection, and addressing everyday concerns.

Insights from the Vedas

While the complex language and ritualistic nature of the Vedas may seem daunting to the modern reader, their core wisdom continues to resonate across time. These ancient texts offer a treasure trove of insights that remain relevant even today.

Understanding the Universe: The Vedas delve into the origin and functioning of the universe, with concepts like "Rita" (cosmic order) and "Karma" (law of cause and effect) forming the basis for the Hindu worldview.

The Art of Ritual: The Vedas provide detailed instructions for performing various rituals and ceremonies. These practices, while evolving, offer a way to connect with the divine and express devotion.

Guiding Principles for Morality: The Vedas emphasize the importance of living a righteous and ethical life. Concepts like Dharma (duty) and Satya (truth) serve as moral compasses, guiding individuals towards right conduct.

The Exploration of Self: Embedded within the Vedas are profound ideas about the nature of reality, the self (Atman), and the connection between the individual and the universal Brahman (ultimate reality).

Lessons From the Vedas

The Vedas resonate with modern minds, offering a treasure trove of ancient wisdom that addresses profound questions about identity, life's purpose, and inner peace. While not everyone reads the Vedas daily, their principles shape Hindu culture, influencing customs, rituals, and perspectives on the world. Here are simple daily practices to integrate this wisdom into our lives.

Perform Prayer and Ceremonies: Incorporate Vedic hymns and mantras into your prayers, rituals, and ceremonies, such as weddings and pujas. This adds a spiritual dimension to these practices and connects you to the ancient tradition.

Embrace Good Values: Find inspiration in the Vedas to lead a virtuous and righteous life. Integrate moral and ethical values from these teachings into your daily conduct, guiding you in making ethical decisions.

Discover Yoga and Meditation: Explore the profound philosophy behind yoga, rooted in Vedic concepts. Embrace practices that lead to self-realization and unity with the divine, promoting physical and mental well-being.

Celebrate Festivals with Meaning: Understand the Vedic connections present in Hindu festivals. During celebrations, consider incorporating recitations of Vedic texts to deepen your connection with the spiritual significance of the occasion.

Reflect on Philosophical Ideas: Engage in contemplation about philosophical ideas from the Vedas, such as the nature of reality and the purpose of life. Use these reflections as a guide for personal growth and understanding the deeper aspects of life.

By incorporating these practices, you can unlock the timeless wisdom of the Vedas and use them as a guide for living a meaningful and fulfilling life. Remember, the vast collection of Hindu scriptures offers a wealth of knowledge waiting to be explored. While some texts delve into complex philosophy and rituals, others provide practical guidance and captivating stories. By approaching these scriptures with an open mind and a curious spirit, you can discover valuable insights that enrich your understanding of the world, yourself, and the divine.

Bhagavad Gita

The Bhagavad Gita is a sacred Hindu scripture that describes a conversation between Lord Krishna and the warrior prince Arjuna on the battlefield just before a great war. Arjuna is confused and morally troubled about fighting.

Insights from the Gita

Krishna counsels Arjuna, imparting wisdom about duty (Dharma), righteousness, and the nature of life and death. He teaches Arjuna about fulfilling one's responsibilities without attachment to the outcomes, the importance of selflessness, and the eternal nature of the soul.

The Bhagavad Gita is part of the Indian epic Mahabharata. Its authorship is attributed to Sage Vyasa, who is traditionally believed to have written the Mahabharata and is also considered the compiler of the Vedas.

Lessons from the Gita

The Bhagavad Gita imparts timeless wisdom, offering guidance on duty, righteousness, and the pursuit of a meaningful life. Its teachings remain relevant, addressing modern challenges with profound insights. Let's explore some lessons from this sacred text.

Detachment with Action (Karma Yoga)

Focus on performing your duties diligently, but remain detached from the desired outcomes. This allows you to act with integrity and avoid the burden of attachment.

Adaptability

Learn to adjust your approach based on changing circumstances without losing your moral compass.

Mind Management

Understand the importance of controlling your mind to make rational decisions.

Work Ethic

Embrace dedication and focus in your work while staying detached from results. Strive for excellence, not just outcomes.

Equality

Recognize the inherent divinity and value in all beings, regardless of their social status or role in life. This fosters a sense of unity and respect.

Inner Peace

Cultivate inner peace amidst life's challenges by incorporating practices like meditation and mindfulness.

Self-Discovery

Strive for self-discovery and personal growth to lead a more fulfilling life.

Balanced Living

Learn the art of balanced living by harmonizing spiritual and worldly pursuits.

In essence, the teachings of the Gita provide timeless wisdom applicable to navigating the complexities of modern life with integrity and purpose.

Ramayana

The Ramayana, a cherished Hindu scripture, beautifully tells the story of Lord Ram, his beloved wife Sita, and his loyal ally Hanuman. Penned by Sage Valmiki, it unfolds Rama's exile, Sita's abduction by the demon king Ravan, and Rama's noble quest to rescue her. A tale is woven with love, honor, sacrifice, and the triumph of righteousness over adversity.

Insights from the Ramayana

In the Ramayana story, the characters of Rama, Sita, Hanuman, and Ravan show different sides of human nature. They teach us about being good, having good relationships, and staying strong even when things are tough. The Ramayana is a guide that helps us understand life's ups and downs with its deep and lasting wisdom.

Compelling Characters, Enduring Lessons

The Ramayana showcases a rich tapestry of characters who embody different facets of human nature.

Rama: The ideal prince, son, and husband. Rama exemplifies the importance of fulfilling one's duty (Dharma), even in the face of immense personal sacrifice.

Sita: Sita, the epitome of a devoted wife, courageously endures hardship with unwavering faith and dignity.

Hanuman: The loyal monkey god Hanuman embodies unwavering devotion and selfless service. His dedication to Rama teaches valuable lessons about loyalty and commitment.

Ravan: The demon king Ravan represents greed, arrogance, and the destructive consequences of succumbing to one's vices.

These characters serve as living metaphors, each offering us invaluable insight.

Lessons from the Ramayana

The Ramayana imparts profound spiritual and ethical lessons that resonate through the ages. It reveals the importance of duty and righteousness, even in the face of adversity, underscoring the essence of Dharma. Through its exploration of familial relationships and loyalty, the epic emphasizes the spiritual significance of respecting loved ones. It powerfully illustrates how virtue and righteousness overcome evil, teaching that integrity and moral strength ultimately prevail. Rama's character teaches you about ethical leadership and wise decision-making, while Hanuman's unwavering devotion and Sita's steadfastness offer lessons in dedication and sacrifice. These characters provide deep spiritual and ethical guidance for your own journey.

Mahabharata

The Mahabharata was composed over centuries, with Its authorship attributed to Sage Vyasa; however, the Mahabharata is a vast work with contributions from various sages and storytellers over time.

Insights from the Mahabharata

The Mahabharata is an ancient Indian epic that vividly depicts human nature. The narrative revolves around a bitter feud between two branches of the same royal family, the Pandavas and the Kauravas, culminating in the Kurukshetra War, a conflict of epic proportions.

The epic is filled with intricate plots, complex characters, and ethical dilemmas. It includes teachings about righteousness, duty, loyalty, and the consequences of actions.

Nestled within the Mahabharata is the Bhagavad Gita, a spiritual discourse delivered by Krishna to the warrior prince Arjuna on the battlefield, discussing duty, righteousness, and the nature of life and death.

Lessons from The Mahabharata

While the war serves as a central plot device, the true brilliance of the Mahabharata lies in the profound lessons it imparts. You learn about the price of greed and arrogance through the Kauravas' downfall, revealing the dangers of unchecked ambition and pride. The epic highlights the importance of righteousness (Dharma), showing how the Pandavas stay true to their path despite immense adversity and deceit. You discover the complexities of duty and responsibility as the characters face challenges involving loyalty, justice, and difficult decisions. The power of unity shines through the Pandavas' strength, illustrating the value of teamwork, cooperation, and family bonds. Lastly, you grasp the consequences of actions, understanding the law of karma and how every action has its effects, both good and bad.

Puranas

The Puranas, another cornerstone of Hindu scriptures, are a vast collection of ancient texts containing stories of gods and goddesses, cosmology, and history. Important Puranas include Vishnu Purana, Shiva Purana, and Bhagavata Purana.

The Puranas were composed over a long period. They don't have a single author, as various sages and scholars have contributed to these texts over time. The traditional belief is that Sage Vyasa is associated with compiling and organizing the Puranas. Still, their creation involves many authors and has evolved through oral and written traditions across ages.

The Puranas are like an ancient library of stories that share wisdom about life, morals, and spirituality. They teach us about good behaviour, the creation of the universe, and the roles of gods and goddesses.

Insights from The Puranas

The rich and intricate narratives of the Puranas contain a treasure trove of valuable lessons and profound knowledge that transcend time. Let's uncover Puranas to learn the insights they provide.

Understanding the Cosmos: The Puranas offer insights into creation stories, the structure of the universe, and the cycles of time. They provide a framework for understanding our place within the cosmos.

The Divine Realm: The stories delve into the lives and characteristics of various gods and goddesses. They provide insights into their roles in the universe and the ways humans can interact with the divine.

Rituals and Traditions: The Puranas detail various rituals, festivals, and practices associated with Hindu traditions. They offer guidance on how to connect with the divine and live a meaningful life.

Cultural Heritage: These ancient stories preserve a rich tapestry of Indian culture, customs, and traditions. They provide insights into the values and beliefs that have shaped society for centuries.

Lessons from the Puranas

The narratives within the Puranas are rich with moral and spiritual lessons. Through these stories, you learn about the profound virtues of honesty, compassion, and respect for elders, which are essential for spiritual growth and ethical living. They guide you in deepening your connection with the divine through sacred rituals and heartfelt devotion. Moreover, they illuminate our cultural heritage and historical roots, offering a deeper understanding of our spiritual values and ancestral wisdom. Each lesson is designed to enrich your journey, fostering a more profound connection with the divine and a greater appreciation of your spiritual heritage.

The First Yoga Discourse/Teaching: A Cosmic Offering

Before delving into this sacred discourse, it is important to understand its context. The following text is a profound dialogue between God Shiva and Goddess Parvati, where Shiva, revered as the first yogi, imparts the fundamental lessons of yoga to Parvati. Shiva lays the foundation of yoga through detailed step-by-step teaching, making this discourse the earliest instruction on the subject. Acknowledging this sacred teaching is crucial, as it highlights the significance of honoring Shiva as the original yoga teacher, preceding all subsequent authors and practitioners of yoga.

On the serene slopes of Mount Kailash, the divine couple, God Shiva and Goddess Parvati, engage in a mystical teaching. Parvati, eager to grasp and teach the world wisdom of yoga, turns to Shiva, the eternal yogi. With tranquil poise, Shiva imparts the essence of the Eight Limbs of Yoga, a step-by-step guide to self-realization.

The first step, Yama, focuses on ethical living. Shiva emphasizes the importance of honesty, compassion, and non-violence – the foundation for a good life. Parvati listens intently and, with utmost devotion, absorbs each teaching.

The lessons progress to Niyama, where Parvati learns about personal discipline and self-purification. Here, Shiva embodies the essence of ascetic practices, demonstrating the power of inner observances.

Moving on, Shiva explains the importance of stable postures (Asana) and breath control (Pranayama). Parvati mirrors Shiva's poised meditation, internalizing the teachings with grace.

The journey continues with concentration (Dharana), meditation (Dhyana), and union with the divine (Samadhi). The divine couple embodies the harmonious union of masculine and feminine energies, a sacred dance symbolizing the profound journey of yoga. In their celestial abode, Shiva and Parvati, cosmic teachers, illuminate the timeless wisdom of the Eight Limbs of Yoga, shaping a sacred dance between the individual soul and cosmic consciousness.

This profound discourse establishes Shiva as the foremost yoga teacher and serves as an eternal source of inspiration for all who seek to understand and practice yoga's true essence. Reflecting on these divine teachings, we honor yoga's origins and reaffirm our connection to its spiritual roots.

Yoga Sutras of Patanjali

A foundational text on yoga philosophy and practices outlining the path of Raja Yoga, authored by Sage Patanjali. The Yoga Sutras discuss the nature -of the mind, the path to inner peace, and spiritual liberation through yoga. They explore the various aspects of yoga, including ethics, meditation, concentration, and attaining a higher state of consciousness.

Patanjali's teachings outline the eightfold path of yoga, known as Ashtanga Yoga. This path includes principles like ethical conduct (Yamas and Niyamas), physical postures (Asanas), breath control (Pranayama), withdrawing senses (Pratyahara), concentration (Dharana), meditation (Dhyana), and ultimately, union with the self (Samadhi).

The Yoga Sutras emphasize the importance of self-discipline, mental focus, moral conduct, and the cultivation of a calm and steady mind through meditation and yoga practices. They guide practitioners toward self-realization, inner peace, and spiritual growth.

In essence, the Yoga Sutras of Patanjali offer a systematic and philosophical approach to yoga practice, encompassing ethical guidelines, physical postures, breath control, and meditation techniques to attain spiritual harmony and self-awareness.

Dharma Shastras

Dharmashastras are ancient texts in Hinduism that discuss moral - and ethical guidelines, duties, laws, and principles for leading a righteous life.

The Dharmashastra texts were composed by various ancient scholars, primarily between the 2nd century BCE and the 6th century CE. Notable authors include Manu, Yajnvalkya, and Narada, among others. They are attributed to being the authors of significant Dharmashastra texts.

Dharmashastra texts cover many topics, such as how to behave, what's right and wrong, laws, and how to live a good life. They - give rules for different social classes, rulers, and individuals, emphasizing good behavior, right living, and order in society. In simple terms, these texts are like guides for living well and doing the right thing, helping people in ancient India—understand how to behave and maintain harmony in society.

Aranyakas and Brahmanas

Aranyakas and Brahmanas are ancient Hindu texts that explain rituals, ceremonies, and deeper meanings behind the Vedic hymns and sacrifices. Wise sages and priests in ancient India crafted the Aranyakas and Brahmanas.

Aranyakas focus more on rituals and ceremonies, while Brahmanas delve into the philosophical and symbolic aspects of these rituals.

काश

Tantra

Tantras are a diverse collection of ancient texts in Hinduism that emerged around the 5th century CE. These texts are like secret manuals, explaining how to do rituals, meditation, and worship of gods spiritually and mystically.

The authors of Tantras remain mostly anonymous. These texts were transmitted orally and passed down through lineages, attributed to divine revelations or spiritual experiences.

They focus on the worship of deities, energy centers (chakras), and methods for achieving spiritual enlightenment. Tantras emphasize the use of mantras, yantras (sacred diagrams), and mudras (gestures) to invoke spiritual energies and attain liberation (moksha).

Note: it's essential to acknowledge that the sacred texts and books of Hinduism mentioned here only scratch the surface of its vast wisdom. Numerous other scriptures and texts exist that are waiting to be explored. Readers are encouraged to delve into the originals to truly grasp the depth and breadth of this ancient tradition, finding enlightenment in the pages of these timeless works.

Chapter 11

Empowering the Next Generation

In the heart of this modern era, we uncover a profound key to preserving our rich Hindu traditions through this book. As we explore its pages, let's not only embrace its wisdom but regard it as a cherished family heirloom. Envision safeguarding this treasure in a secure vault, embedding it in a virtual time capsule, or designating a special place in our digital realm. By doing so, we provide our children with more than just a guide; we offer them a precious family legacy that encapsulates the essence of Hindu traditions. Whether preserved in print or digitally, this legacy ensures that our cultural heritage will continue to illuminate the hearts of future generations.

Preserving and transmitting Hindu Heritage involves passing down the sacred threads of rituals, stories, and cultural practices from one generation to the next. Let's explore effective strategies to thoughtfully pass down these invaluable traditions to future generations, ensuring their enduring relevance, richness, and cultural significance.

Engage in Traditions

Involve all family members, especially children, in rituals and festivals, showing them to take pride in their heritage. Gather together to guide everyone through traditions, rituals, festivals, and puja. These heartfelt interactions create shared experiences, bridging past and future generations. Embrace curiosity, active participation, and a deeper understanding of the values and customs that enrich your family's traditions.

Hands-On Wisdom

Engage in interactive sessions where elders impart hands-on knowledge, such as guiding rituals, prayers, and chants. For the next festival, take the lead under their guidance. Enjoy celebrations with elders guiding the way, and take photos and videos to remember these special moments as you prepare to lead in the future.

Cultural Explorations

Embark on journeys together to explore various temples and immerse yourselves in their spiritual and cultural significance. Attend cultural events and visit heritage sites to deepen your understanding of traditions, history, and the essence of Hinduism along the way.

Technological Integration

Use technology as a powerful bridge to craft, save, and share stories about your family's history, traditions, and personal tales, ensuring they last. Moreover, it can be utilized to gather family members virtually for religious ceremonies or gatherings, weaving connections across distances.

Preserving and transmitting Hindu heritage is about ensuring that the sacred threads of cultural practices flow seamlessly from one generation to the next. As we embark on this journey, let us commit to nurturing these timeless practices, ensuring that they continue to enrich the lives and hearts of those who come after us.

Passing the Torch

In this book, I aim to convey the essence of our cultural and ritual practices while acknowledging the pivotal role elders play as torchbearers. Despite my efforts, errors may occur, and I humbly ask for forgiveness for any inadvertent mistakes. The practices shared here stem from the wisdom imparted by my ancestors. I urge readers to approach these teachings with respect and humility, seeking guidance from their own family and elders.

In the quiet moments spent with these insightful chapters, we've explored the depths of our heritage and woven stronger threads that bind us across time.

As we draw the curtains on this heartfelt journey through the pages of our shared wisdom, picture the torch of Hinduism passing gently from the hands of one generation to the next. Together, we carry forward the luminous flame of Hinduism, ensuring that its brilliance continues to radiate in the hearts and minds of those yet to walk this path.

Sacred Notes

www.ingramcontent.com/pod-product-compliance
Lightning Source LLC
Chambersburg PA
CBHW020431130626
46549CB00001B/83